D1741093

# POETRY OF THE SCOTTISH BORDERS

Edited by
**ALEX CAMERON**

Illustrated by Gordon Home

ALBYN PRESS LTD
Edinburgh

Made and printed
in Scotland
and published by
ALBYN PRESS LTD
2 & 3 Abbeymount
Edinburgh 8

The illustrations by Gordon Home are taken from *The Charm
of the Scott Country* by Rev. James Baikie, F.R.S.A., published
by A & C Black Limited. They are reproduced by courtesy of
the publishers.

# CONTENTS

# PREFACE

I present this little anthology of Border Poetry with the earnest hope of awaking a new awareness in our generation of the great heritage we have, and which we would do well to preserve, not only for ourselves but for our children yet unborn. The love of poetry waxes and wanes as the fashions change, and the moods of men, but I really believe that here is something which is abiding and real in this transient age. Some would say that the learning of poetry off by heart is not for this modern era, but this I would simply say: it is a great enjoyment, to someone who is growing older, to bring to mind verses learned at school many years ago, which in turn open up vistas to the inward eye so that the old landmarks come alive again!

The true poet is a gifted being and can see things that lesser mortals can but look at and wonder. He can turn two lines and make your heart beat a little faster, and you wonder why you couldn't do the same. Perhaps O' Shaughnessy has the right of it:

> We are the music makers,
> We are the dreamers of dreams,
> Wandering by lone sea-breakers,
> And sitting by desolate streams; —
> World losers and world forsakers,
> On whom the pale moon gleams:
> We are its movers and shakers
> Of the world for ever, it seems.
> One man with a dream at pleasure,
> Shall go forth and conquer a crown;
> And three with a new song's measure
> Can trample a kingdom down.

I have endeavoured to select poetry about the people or the countryside, and the greatest difficulty is to decide what to leave out! Sir Walter Scott dominates the scene by sheer volume of work, but he did so much to secure for posterity all that was noble and valiant in literature. I have left out much of his work, and from *Marmion* have quoted only "Young Lochinvar . . .", but I have selected a fair amount from *The Lay of the Last Minstrel* — a poem which is timeless and still moves us today.

I confess to a great personal liking of J. B. Selkirk. I think his poem on Flodden is a masterpiece.

One is greatly indebted to men of the past for their careful analysis and criticism: men like Professor Veitch, Borland, Crockett and Aytoun, and many others whose love of the Borders has been an abiding passion which in turn produced some great literature.

For permission to use poetry from the pen of Will Ogilvie, I am grateful to his executors; to others who have encouraged this work and helped with useful criticism, I am indebted.

A. C.

# INTRODUCTION

The Borders have a natural beauty unsurpassed in the land, which, with its history of feuding and romance, have made it rich soil indeed for the fertile mind. Poets and writers have germinated fast in these parts and have left us a vast storehouse of song and story.

For hundreds of years the Borderland was an almost constant scene of battle and plunder, and when its people weren't actually engaged in fighting they were licking their wounds and preparing for the next foray. When the English had had just about enough, the Scots would ease off for a while and would simply take to fighting each other. Occasionally the king would come down from Edinburgh to sort them out a bit. James IV and his son James V in turn took it out on not a few Border worthies. Johnny Armstrong, Cockburn and Scott . . . These fiery encounters inspired some of the finest ballads and poems. It would seem that nearly all of this poetry is shrouded in sorrow: "The Widow's Lament", "Willie's Drowned in Yarrow", "The Douglas Tragedy", "The Flowers of the Forest" . . . Flodden had a devastating effect on the whole of the Borders; whole towns harried of the breadwinners. The land wept and groaned to bury its dead and hide its maimed. The sadness is still with us today — witness the moving ceremony at our Common Ridings and feel the lump in your throat when they play the "Lilting" and you'll know that it's in your very bones.

Sir Walter Scott was most richly endowed to write poetry and collect ballads. The goings on in the Borders suited his temperament. Indeed, I think Hogg has put him just where he belongs when he says:

> For war thy boardly frame was born
> For battle shout and bugle horn;
> Chance marred the path, or Heaven's decree;
> How blessed for Scotland and for me.

But his lameness from early youth never hindered him in any way: he was worth any two men when he was on a horse.

Some have said that, when the ballads and songs of the minstrels were written down by Scott, Leyden and others, it was the end of the singing and memorising. This could be, but one shudders to think of what would have happened to the ballads had they continued to be handed down by oral tradition to this day. We must accept that errors are there, which experts will carefully point out, yet if you look at the picture as a whole it is exciting, expansive and yearningly expressive.

In my section on Scott I have selected quite a lot, as already mentioned, from *The Lay of the Last Minstrel*. I deliberately did not touch on the story, but rather chose those parts which express feelings about the participants and the countryside. I love the closing stanzas of the poem where it encompasses all the richness of Yarrow, its beauty, its sounds, its sadness — Newark Tower, Sweet Bowhill and the throstles singing in Harehead-shaw.

I have quoted one of the three poems which Wordsworth wrote on Yarrow. He had obviously been fed on the milk of the land by Scott long before he came to see the Valley.

> And is this — Yarrow? — this the stream
> Of which my fancy cherished?

My heart doesn't quite beat with his rhyme. Perhaps it is because he writes from the outside looking in.

J. B. Selkirk, on the other hand, excites the imagination, especially in his poem on Flodden. Here is pathetic majesty in verse, heartrending in parts:

> Then I turn to sister Jean
> And my airms aboot her twine,
> And I kiss her sleepless een
> For her heart's as sair as mine.

4

J. B.'s poem on Ettrick is great reading, though a bit long. It has many quotable parts, from the "Border Burn" to the "Transplanting o' Auld Folk".

It has been said that anything up to a thousand poets have written about Yarrow; as one of the early poets put it, "Was ever a valley so besung?" I have tried to spread the interest around as many parts of the Borders as possible but Yarrow does seem to attract the poets.

"Kilmeny" is a lovely poem and perhaps that alone ensures a place in history for the Ettrick Shepherd, James Hogg. For an untutored man he wrote at tremendous length. Some of his other poems which I have included portray the real man inside, especially when he addresses his dog Hector.

Roger Quin, in his poem "The Borderland", gives us a racy view of the Borders and fairly bubbles over when he "Gazes on Scotland's Eden, from the spur of Gala Hill". Unfortunately most of Quin's work appears to have been written on the backs of envelopes or in letters to friends and I think many a jewel has been lost to us for ever.

John Leyden was perhaps a greater linguist than he was a poet. His *Scenes from Infancy* is a lengthy piece of work, some of it rather hard going I must confess. He starts well, describing a scene, but then it fades from view and something else takes its place. A fascinating man, nevertheless, in many ways . . .

Will Ogilvie from the Kelso "airt" writes some nostalgic poetry all the way from Australia. "The Deil's Mitten" is my favourite. "Smailholm Tower", (the scene of Sir Walter Scott's childhood) is illustrative of the way in which the finer qualities of a man have a common root in time, where early associations determine what we shall love and revere.

Willie Laidlaw has a loving poem in "Lucy's Flittin' ", leaving a lot of unanswered questions.

The ballads, about which much has been written in the

5

past, are just another part of our rich heritage: "The Outlaw Murray", telling of the powerful castle dweller taking on the King himself; "The Dowie Dens", talked about the world over; "The Douglas Tragedy", describing lovers dying together, and the rose and the briar which twined out of their graves in St Mary's Kirk . . . Armstrong and Cockburn in turn yield their own variations to the theme, blended with Aytoun's "Willie's Drowned in Yarrow" and Jean Elliot's "Flowers o' the Forest", the whole rising to a crescendo of music and story, blending mountain and river, lover and warrior, life and death — and, pervading all, the sweet sadness that engulfs you as you walk through the land again.

*Scott's favourite view*
*The Eildons & The Tweed*
*from above Bemersyde*

# MINSTRELSY OF THE SCOTTISH BORDER

## THE OUTLAW MURRAY

Ettricke Foreste is a feir foreste,
    In it grows manie a semelie trie;
There's hart and hynde, and dae and rae,
    And of a' wilde beastis grete plentie.

There's a feir castelle, bigged wi' lyme and stane;
    O! gin it stands not pleasauntlie!
In the forefront o' that castelle feir,
    Twa unicorns are bra' to see;
There's the picture of a knighte, and a ladye bright,
    And the grene hollin abune their brie.

There an Outlaw keepis five hundred men;
    He keepis a royalle cumpanie!
His merryemen are a' in ae liverye clad,
    O' the Lincome grene saye gaye to see;
He and his ladye in purple clad,
    O! gin they lived not royallie!

Word is gane to our nobil King,
    In Edinburgh, where that he lay,
That there was an Outlaw in Ettricke Foreste,
    Counted him nought, nor a' his courtrie gay.

"I make a vowe," then the gude King said,
    "Unto the man that deir bought me,
I'se either be King of Ettricke Foreste,
    Or King of Scotlande that Outlaw sall be!"

Then spak the lord, hight Hamilton,
    And to the nobil King said he,
"My sovereign prince, sum counsell take,
    First at your nobilis, syne at me.

7

"I redd ye, send yon braw Outlaw till,
    And see gif your man cum will he:
Desyre him cum and be your man,
    And hald of you yon Foreste frie.

"Gif he refuses to do that,
    We'll conquess baith his landis and he!
Or else, we'll throw his castell down,
    And make a widowe o' his gaye ladye."

The King then call'd a gentleman,
    James Boyd, the Earl of Arran (his brother was he);
When James he cam before the King,
    He knelit before him on his kné.

"Wellcum, James Boyd!" said our nobil King;
    "A message ye maun gang for me;
Ye maun hye to Ettricke Foreste,
    To yon Outlaw, where bydeth he:

"Ask him of whom he haldis his landis,
    Or man, wha may his master be,
And desyre him cum, and be my man,
    And hald of me yon Foreste frie.

"To Edinburgh to cum and gang,
    His safe warrant I shall gie;
And gif he refuses to do that,
    We'll conquess baith his landis and he.

"Thou mayst vow I'll cast his castell down,
    And mak a widowe o' his gaye ladye;
I'll hang his merryemen, payr by payr,
    In ony frith where I may them see."

James Boyd tuik his leave o' the nobil King,
    To Ettricke Foreste feir cam he;
Down Birkendale Brae when that he cam,
    He saw the feir Foreste wi' his ee.

Baith dae and rae, and hart and hynde,
  And of a' wilde beastis great plentie;
He heard the bows that bauldly ring,
  And arrows whidderan' hym near bi.

Of that feir castell he got a sight;
  The like he neir saw wi' his ee!
On the forefront o' that castell feir,
  Twa unicorns were gaye to see;
The picture of a knight, and lady bright,
  And the grene hollin abune their brie.

Thereat he spyed five hundred men,
  Shuting with bows on Newark Lee;
They were a' in ae livery clad,
  O' the Lincome grene sae gaye to see.

His men were a' clad in the grene,
  The knight was armed capapie,
With a bended bow, on a milk-white steed;
  And I wot they ranked right bonilie.

Thereby Boyd kend he was master man,
  And serv'd him in his ain degré.
"God mot thee save, brave Outlaw Murray!
  Thy ladye, and all thy chyvalrie!"
"Marry, thou's wellcum, gentleman,
  Some king's messenger thou seemis to be."

"The King of Scotlande sent me here,
  And, gude Outlaw, I am sent to thee;
I wad wot of whom ye hald your landis,
  Or man, wha may thy master be?"

"Thir landis are MINE!" the Outlaw said;
  "I ken nae King in Christentie;
Frae Soudron I this Foreste wan,
  Whan the King nor his knightis were not to see."

"He desyres you'l cum to Edinburgh,
    And hauld of him this Foreste frie;
And, gif ye refuse to do this,
    He'll conquess baith thy landis and thee.
He hath vow'd to cast thy castell down,
    And mak a widowe o' thy gaye ladye;

"He'll hang thy merryemen, payr by payr,
    In ony frith where he may them finde."
"Ay, by my troth!" the Outlaw said,
    "Than wald I thinke me far behinde."

James Boyd tuik his leave o' the Outlaw kene,
    To Edinburgh boun is he;
When James he cam before the King,
    He knelit lowlie on his kné.

"Wellcum, James Boyd!" seyd our nobil King;
    "What Foreste is Ettricke Foreste frie?"
"Ettricke Foreste is the feirest foreste
    That evir man saw wi' his ee.

"There's the dae, the rae, the hart, the hynde,
    And of a' wild beastis grete plentie;
There's a pretty castell of lyme and stane,
    O gif it standis not pleasauntlie!
There's in the forefront o' that castell,
    Twa unicorns sae bra' to see;
There's the picture of a knight, and a ladye bright,
    Wi' the grene hollin abune their brie.

"There the Outlaw keepis five hundred men,
    He keepis a royalle cumpanie!
His merryemen in ae livery clad,
    O' the Lincome grene sae gaye to see:
He and his ladye in purple clad;
    O! gin they live not royallie!

10

"He says, yon Foreste is his awin;
    He wan it frae the Southronie;
Sae as he wan it, sae will he keep it,
    Contrair all kingis in Christentie."

"Gar warn me Perthshire, and Angus baith;
    Fife up and down, and the Louthians three,
And graith my horse!" said the nobil King,
    For to Ettricke Foreste hie will I me."

Then word is gane the Outlaw till,
    In Ettricke Foreste, where dwelleth he,
That the King was cuming to his cuntrie,
    To conquess baith his landis and he.

The King was cuming thro' Caddon Ford,
    And full five thousand men was he;
They saw the derke Foreste them before,
    They thought it awsome for to see.

"Desyre him mete thee at Permanscore,
    And bring four in his cumpanie;
Five erles sall gang yoursell befor,
    Gude cause that you suld honour'd be.

"And, gif he refuses to do that,
    We'll conquess baith his landis and he;
There sall nevir a Murray, after him,
    Hald land in Ettricke Foreste frie."

"Wellcum, James Pringle of Torsonse!
    A message ye maun gang for me;
Ye maun gae to yon Outlaw Murray,
    Surely where bauldly bideth he.

"Bid him mete me at Permanscore,
    And bring four in his cumpanie;
Five erles sall cum wi' mysell,
    Gude reason I suld honour'd be."

11

When that they cam before the King,
  They fell before him on their kne—
"Grant mercie, mercie, nobil King!
  E'en for his sake that dyed on tree,

"I'll give thee the keys of my castell,
  Wi' the blessing o' my gaye ladye,
Gin thou'lt mak me sheriffe of this Foreste,
  And a' my offspring after me."

"Wilt thou give me the keys of thy castell,
  Wi' the blessing of thy gaye ladye?
I'se mak thee sheriffe of Ettricke Foreste,
  Surely while upwards grows the tree;
If you be not traitour to the King,
  Forfaulted sall thou nevir be.

"Will your merryemen amend their lives?
  And a' their pardons I graunt thee —
Now, name thy landis where'er they lie,
  And I here RENDER them to thee."

"Fair Philiphaugh is mine by right,
  And Lewinshope still mine shall be;
Newark, Foulshiels, and Tinnies baith,
  My bow and arrow purchased me.

"And I have native steads to me,
  The Newark Lee and Hangingshaw;
I have mony steads in the Foreste shaw,
  But them by name I dinna knaw."

The keys o' the castell he gave the King,
  Wi' the blessing of his fair ladye;
He was made sheriffe of Ettricke Foreste,
  Surely while upward grows the tree;
And if he was na traitour to the King
  Forfaulted he suld nevir be.

Wha ever heard, in ony times,
    Sicken an Outlaw in his degré,
Sic favour get before a King,
    As did the OUTLAW MURRAY of the Foreste frie?

*Sir Walter Scott's*
*writing-table & chair*
*at Abbotsford*

# THE DOWIE DENS OF YARROW

Late at e'en, drinking the wine,
   And ere they paid the lawing,
They set a combat them between,
   To fight it in the dawing.

"O stay at hame, my noble lord!
   O stay at hame, my marrow!
My cruel brother will you betray
   On the dowie houms of Yarrow."

"O fare ye weel, my ladye gaye!
   O fare ye weel, my Sarah!
For I maun gae, though I ne'er return,
   Frae the dowie banks o' Yarrow."

She kiss'd his cheek, she kaim'd his hair,
   As oft she had done before, O;
She belted him with his noble brand,
   And he's awa' to Yarrow.

As he gaed up the Tennies bank,
   I wot he gaed wi' sorrow,
Till, down in a den, he spied nine arm'd men,
   On the dowie houms of Yarrow.

"O come ye here to part your land,
   The bonnie Forest thorough?
Or come ye here to wield your brand,
   On the dowie houms of Yarrow?"

"I come not here to part my land,
   And neither to beg nor borrow;
I come to wield my noble brand,
   On the bonnie banks of Yarrow.

"Now, haud your tongue, my daughter dear!
　　For a' this breeds but sorrow;
I'll wed ye to a better lord,
　　Than him ye lost on Yarrow."

"O haud your tongue, my father dear,
　　Ye mind me but of sorrow;
A fairer rose did never bloom
　　Than now lies cropp'd on Yarrow."

*Kelso Abbey
& Bridge*

"If I see all, ye're nine to ane;
    And that's an unequal marrow;
Yet I will fight, while lasts my brand,
    On the bonnie banks of Yarrow."

Four he has hurt, and five has slain,
    On the bloody braes of Yarrow,
Till that stubborn knight came him behind,
    And ran his bodie thorough.

"Gae hame, gae hame, good-brother John,
    And tell your sister Sarah,
To come and lift her noble lord;
    He's sleepin sound on Yarrow." —

"Yestreen I dream'd a dolefu' dream;
    I fear there will be sorrow!
I dream'd, I pu'd the heather green,
    Wi' my true love, on Yarrow.

"O gentle wind, that bloweth south,
    From where my love repaireth,
Convey a kiss from his dear mouth,
    And tell me how he fareth!

"But in the glen strive armèd men;
    They've wrought me dole and sorrow;
They've slain — the comliest knight they've slain —
    He bleeding lies on Yarrow."

As she sped down yon high high hill,
    She gaed wi' dole and sorrow,
And in the den spied ten slain men,
    On the dowie banks of Yarrow.

She kiss'd his cheek, she kaim'd his hair,
    She search'd his wounds all thorough;
She kiss'd them, till her lips grew red,
    On the dowie houms of Yarrow.

# JOHNIE ARMSTRANG

Sum speikis of lords, sum speikis of lairds,
 And sic lyke men of hie degrie;
Of a gentle man I sing a sang,
 Sum tyme call'd Laird of Gilnockie.

The King he wrytes a luving letter,
 With his ain hand sae tenderly,
And he hath sent it to Johnie Armstrang,
 To cum and speik with him speedily.

The Eliots and Armstrangs did convene;
 They were a gallant cumpanie —
"We'll ride and meit our lawful King,
 And bring him safe to Gilnockie.

"Make kinnen and capon ready, then,
 And venison in great pentie;
We'll welcum here our royal King;
 I hope he'll dine at Gilnockie!"

They ran their horse on the Langholm howm,
 And brak their spears wi' mickle main;
The ladies lukit frae their loft windows —
 "God bring our men weel back agen!"

When Johnie cam before the King,
 W' a' his men sae brave to see,
The King he movit his bonnet to him;
 He ween'd he was a King as weel as he.

"May I find grace, my sovereign liege,
 Grace for my loyal men and me?
For my name it is Johnie Armstrang,
 And subject of yours, my liege," said he.

17

"Away, away thou traitor strang!
  Out o' my sight soon mayst thou be!
I grantit nevir a traitor's life,
  And now I'll not begin wi' thee."

"Grant me my life, my liege, my King!
  And a bonny gift I'll gie to thee —
Full four-and-twenty milk-white steids,
  Were a' foaled in ae yeir to me.

"I'll gie thee a' these milk-white steids,
  That prance and nicker at a speir;
And as mickle gude Inglish gilt,
  As four of their braid backs dow bear."

"Away, away, thou traitor strang!
  Out o' my sight soon mayst thou be!
I grantit nevir a traitor's life,
  And now I'll not begin wi' thee!"

"Grant me my life, my liege, my King!
  And a bonny gift I'll gie to thee —
Gude four-and-twenty ganging mills,
  That gang thro' a' the yeir to me.

"These four-and-twenty mills complete,
  Sall gang for thee thro' a' the yeir;
And as mickle of gude reid wheit,
  As a' their happers dow to bear."

"Away, away, thou traitor strang!
  Out o' my sight soon mayst thou be!
I grantit nevir a traitor's life,
  And now I'll not begin wi' thee!".

"Grant me my life, my liege, my King!
  And a great gift I'll gie to thee —
Bauld four-and-twenty sisters' sons,
  Sall for thee fecht, tho' a should flee!"

"Away, away, thou traitor strang!
    Out o' my sight soon mayst thou be!
I grantit nevir a traitor's life,
    And now I'll not begin wi' thee!"

"Grant me my life, my liege, my King!
    And a brave gift I'll gie to thee —
All between heir and Newcastle town
    Sall pay their yeirly rent to thee."

"Away, away, thou traitor strang!
    Out o' my sight soon mayst thou be!
I grantit nevir a traitor's life,
    And now I'll not begin wi' thee!"

"Ye lied, ye lied, now, King," he says,
    "Altho' a King and Prince ye be!
For I've luved naething in my life,
    I weel dare say it, but honesty —

"Save a fat horse, and a fair woman,
    Twa bonny dogs to kill a deir;
But England suld have found me meal and mault,
    Gif I had lived this hundred yeir!

"She suld have found me meal and mault,
    And beif and mutton in a' plentie;
But nevir a Scots wyfe could have said,
    That e'er I skaith'd her a pure flee.

"To seik het water beneith cauld ice,
    Surely it is a greit folie —
I have asked grace at a graceless face,
    But there is nane for my men and me!

"But, had I kenn'd ere I cam frae hame,
    How thou unkind wadst been to me!
I wad have keepit the Border syde,
    In spite of all thy force and thee.

19

"Wist England's King that I was ta'en,
     O gin a blythe man he wad be!
For anes I slew his sister's son,
     And on his breist bane brak a trie."

John wore a girdle about his middle,
     Inbroidered ower wi' burning gold,
Bespangled wi' the same metal;
     Maist beautiful was to behold.

There hang nine targats at Johnie's hat,
     And ilk ane worth three hundred pound —
"What wants that knave that a King suld have,
     But the sword of honour and the crown!

"Oh whair got thou these targats, Johnie,
     That blink sae brawly abune thy brie?"
"I gat them in the field fechting,
     Where, cruel King, thou durst not be.

"Had I my horse, and harness guide,
     And riding as I wont be,
It suld have been tauld this hundred yeir,
     The meeting of my King and me!

"God be with thee, Kirsty, my brother!
     Lang live thou Laird of Mangertoun!
Lang mayst thou live on the Border syde,
     Ere thou see thy brother ride up and down!

"And God be with thee, Kirsty, my son,
     Where thou sits on thy nurse's knee!
But and thou live this hundred yeir,
     Thy father's better thou'lt nevir be.

"Farewell! my bonny Gilnock hall,
     Where on Esk side thou standest stout!
Gif I had lived but seven yeirs mair,
     I wad hae gilt thee round about."

20

John murdered was at Carlinrigg,
   And all his gallant cumpanie;
But Scotland's heart was ne'er sae wae,
   To see sae mony brave men die —

Because they saved their countrey deir
   Frae Englishmen! Nane were sae bauld,
While Johnie lived on the Border syde,
   Nane of them durst cum neir his hauld.

*Newark Castle*
*Yarrow*

# THE LAMENT OF THE BORDER WIDOW

My love he built me a bonny bower,
    And clad it a' wi' lilye flour;
A brawer bower ye ne'er did see,
    Than my true love he built for me.

There came a man, by middle day,
    He spied his sport, and went away;
And brought the King that very night,
    Who brake my bower, and slew my knight.

He slew my knight, to me sae dear,
    He slew my knight, and poin'd his gear;
My servants all for life did flee,
    And left me in extremitie.

I sew'd his sheet, making my mane;
    I watched the corpse, myself alane;
I watch'd his body night and day;
    No living creature came that way.

I took his body on my back,
    And whiles I gaed, and whiles I sat;
I digg'd a grave, and laid him in,
    And happ'd him with the sod sae green.

But think na ye my heart was sair,
    When I laid the moul' on his yellow hair;
O think na ye my heart was wae,
    When I turn'd about, away to gae?

Nae living man I'll love again,
    Since that my lovely knight is slain;
Wi' ae lock of his yellow hair
    I'll chain my heart for evermair.

# THE DOUGLAS TRAGEDY

"Rise up, rise up, now, Lord Douglas," she says,
   "And put on your armour so bright;
Let it never be said that a daughter of thine
   Was married to a lord under night.

"Rise up, rise up, my seven bold sons,
   And put on your armour so bright,
And take better care of your youngest sister,
   For your eldest's awa' the last night."

He's mounted her on a milk-white steed,
   And himself on a dapple grey,
With a bugelet horn hung down by his side,
   And lightly they rode away.

Lord William lookit o'er his left shoulder,
   To see what he could see,
And there he spy'd her seven brethren bold,
   Come riding o'er the lee.

"Light down, light down, Lady Marg'ret," he said,
   "And hold my steed in your hand,
Until that against your seven brethren bold,
   And your father, I mak a stand."

She held his steed in her milk-white hand,
   And never shed one tear,
Until she saw her seven brethren fa',
   And her father hard fighting, who lov'd her so dear.

"O hold your hand, Lord William!" she said
   "For your strokes they are wondrous sair;
True lovers I can get many a ane,
   But a father I can never get mair."

O she's ta'en out her handkerchief,
   It was o' the holland sae fine,
And aye she dighted her father's bloody wounds,
   That were redder than the wine.

"O chuse, O chuse, Lady Marg'ret, " he said,
   "O whether will ye gang or bide?"
"I'll gang, I'll gang, Lord William," she said
   "For ye have left me no other guide."

He's lifted her on a milk-white steed,
   And himself on a dapple grey,
With a bugelet horn hung down by his side,
   And slowly they baith rade away.

O they rade on, and on they rade,
   And a' by the light of the moon,
Until they came to yon wan water,
   And there they lighted down.

The lighted down to tak a drink
   Of the spring that ran sae clear;
And down the stream ran his gude heart's blood,
   And sair she 'gan to fear.

"Hold up, hold up, Lord William," she says,
   "For I fear that you are slain!"
"Tis naething but the shadow of my scarlet cloak,
   That shines in the water sae plain."

O they rade on, and on they rade,
   And a' by the light of the moon,
Until they cam to his mother's ha' door,
   And there they lighted down.

"Get up, get up, lady mother, " he says,
   "Get up, and let me in! —
Get up, get up, lady mother," he says,
   "For this night my fair lady I've win.

"O mak my bed, lady mother," he says,
   "O mak it braid and deep!
And lay Lady Marg'ret close at my back,
   And the sounder I will sleep."

Lord William was dead lang ere midnight,
   Lady Marg'ret lang ere day —
And all true lovers that go thegither,
   May they have mair luck than they!

Lord William was buried in St Marie's kirk,
   Lady Margaret in Marie's quire;
Out o' the lady's grave grew a bonny red rose,
   And out o' the knight's a brier.

And they twa met, and they twa plat,
   And fain they wad be near;
And a' the warld might ken right weel,
   They were twa lovers dear.

But bye and rade the Black Douglas,
   And wow but he was rough!
For he pull'd up the bonny brier,
   And flang'd in St Marie's Loch.

# WILLIE'S DROWNED IN YARROW

"Willie's rare and Willie's fair,
  And Willie's wondrous bonny,
And Willie's hecht to marry me,
  Gin e'er he married ony.

"Yestreen I made my bed fu' braid,
  This night I'll make it narrow,
For a' the live long winter night
  I'll lie twin'd of my marrow.

"O gentle wind that bloweth south,
  From where my love repaireth,
Convey a kiss from his dear mouth,
  And tell me how he fareth.

"O tell sweet Willie to come doun,
  And bid him no be cruel,
And tell him no to break the heart
  Of his love and only jewel.

"O tell sweet Willie to come doun,
  And hear the mavis singing;
And see the birds on ilka bush,
  And the leaves around them hinging.

"O cam' ye by yon water side?
  Pu'd ye the rose or lily?
Or cam' ye by yon meadow green?
  Or saw ye my sweet Willie?"

She sought him east, she sought him west,
  She sought him braid and narrow;
Syne, in the cleaving of a craig,
  She fand him drown'd in Yarrow.

# JEAN ELLIOT (1727–1805)

*Not a great deal is known about Miss Jean Elliot, but this much we do know: she wrote a song which has had an abiding effect on us all. Jean was the third daughter of the 2nd Baronet of Minto, of good Border stock. Born in 1727, she died at Mount Teviot, her brother's home, in 1805. She has been described as having an aristocratic bearing and of "possessing a sensible face, a slender and well shaped figure"; she remained unmarried all her life.*

*Professor Veitch relates how one evening Miss Elliott was returning home from a party with her brother Gilbert, when they became deeply engaged in conversation about the Battle of Flodden. He light heartedly suggested to Jean that she write a poem about Scotland's tragic day: there and then she proceeded to do so, choosing a tune which was well known at the time and weaving her words into it. From that fateful night emerged that immortal song with the haunting tune, "The Flowers of the Forest". Played on kingly occasions of grief and times of National disaster and lamenting, it has become yet another part of our rich heritage.*

# THE FLOWERS OF THE FOREST

*Jean Elliot*

I've heard them lilting, at the ewe-milking,
   Lasses a' lilting, before dawn of day;
But now they are moaning on ilka green loaning;
   The flowers of the forest are a' wede awae.

At bughts, in the morning, nae blythe lads are scorning;
   Lasses are lonely, and dowie, and wae;
Nae daffing, nae gabbing, but sighing and sabbing;
   Ilk ane lifts her leglin, and hies her awae.

In har'st, at the shearing, nae youths now are jeering;
   Bandsters are runkled, and lyart or gray;
At fair, or at preaching, nae wooing, nae fleeching;
   The flowers of the forest are a' wede awae.

At e'en, in the gloaming, nae younkers are roaming
   'Bout stacks with the lasses at bogle to play;
But ilk maid sits dreary, lamenting her deary —
   The flowers of the forest are weded awae.

Dool and wae for the order, sent our lads to the Border!
   The English for ance, by guile wan the day:
The flowers of the forest that fought aye the foremost,
   The prime of our land, are cauld in the clay.

We'll hear nae mair lilting, at the ewe-milking;
   Women and bairns are heartless and wae,
Sighing and moaning on ilka green loaning —
   The flowers of the forest are a' wede awae.

# JAMES HOGG (1770–1835)

## THE ETTRICK SHEPHERD

*Born at Ettrickhall near to Ettrick Kirk in 1770, James Hogg died at the age of sixty-five on his farm, Altrive, in Yarrow, on November 21st, 1835. Hunger and poverty dogged his footsteps from the day he was born. At the age of seven he was herding cows for the princely sum of a ewe lamb and a pair of shoes — the reward for six months' labour. He did not go to school for more than six months in his entire life — but that was not uncommon for the poor at that time.*

*His early reading was confined to the Bible and the Shorter Catechism. His mother was a great ballad-singer and a story-teller and at home the poet found early inspiration which in later years flourished and brought him the praise of kings and the feting of ladies.*

*As a handsome young shepherd at the age of twenty, herding at Blackhouse in Yarrow, Hogg first felt poetic stirrings as his muse came upon him. Sitting on the hillside with his sheep and his dog Hector, he would take a little phial of ink out of his pocket and cut a quill and there write the poetry that we read today, while the skylark was singing, the heather blooming and the fairies "keeking" out from behind the grasses.*

*Sir Walter Scott was his close friend — Hogg helped him to collect old ballads for the* Border Minstrelsy *— as were Leyden and Christopher North, and he conducted Wordsworth on his tour of the Valley.*

*He loved life and feared death; he was fond of a night in Tibbie Shiel's Inn with boon companions. A pleasing monument to him stands at the head of St Mary's Loch, across from the inn. The inscription reads: "He taught the wandering winds to sing." Just so — he did, indeed. Buried in Ettrick Churchyard, near the place of his birth, he lies in tranquillity beside Tibbie Shiel and Thomas Boston.*

29

# KILMENY

*James Hogg*

Bonnie Kilmeny gaed up the glen;
   But it wasna to meet Duneira's men,
Nor the rosy monk of the isle to see,
   For Kilmeny was pure as pure could be.
It was only to hear the yorlin sing,
   And pu' the cress-flower round the spring;
The scarlet hypp and the hind-berrye,
   And the nest that hung frae the hazel tree;
For Kilmeny was pure as pure could be.
   But lang may her minny look o'er the wa';
And lang may she seek i' the greenwood shaw;
   Lang the laird o' Duneira blame,
And lang, lang greet or Kilmeny come hame!

When many a day had come and fled,
   When grief grew calm, and hope was dead,
When mass for Kilmeny's soul had been sung,
   When the bedes-man had pray'd and the dead-bell rung,
Late, late in a gloamin', when all was still,
   When the fringe was red on the westlin' hill,
The wood was sere, the moon i' the wane,
   The reek o' the cot hung o'er the plain,
Like a little wee cloud in the world its lane;
   When the ingle lowed wi' an eiry leme —
Late, late in the gloamin' Kilmeny came hame!

"Kilmeny, Kilmeny, where have you been?
   Lang hae we sought baith holt and dene;
By burn, by ford, by greenwood tree,
   Yet you are halesome and fair to see.
Where gat ye that joup o' the lily sheen?
   That bonnie snood o' the birk sae green?
And these roses, the fairest that ever were seen?
   Kilmeny, Kilmeny, where have you been?"

Kilmeny look'd up wi' a lovely grace,
　　But nae smile was seen on Kilmeny's face;
As still was her look, and as still was her e'e,
　　As the stillness that lay on the emerant lea,
Or the mist that sleeps on a waveless sea.
　　For Kilmeny had been, she kenned not where,
And Kilmeny had seen what she could not declare,
　　Kilmeny had been where the cock never crew,
Where the rain never fell, and the wind never blew.
　　But it seemed as the harp of the sky had rung,
And the airs of heaven played round her tongue,
　　When she spoke of the lovely forms she had seen,
And a land where sin had never been;
　　A land of love and a land of light,
Withouten sun, or moon, or night;
　　Where the river swa'd a living stream,
And the light a pure and cloudless beam;
　　The land of vision, it would seem,
A still, an everlasting dream.

In yon green wood there is a waik,
　　And in that waik there is a wene,
And in that wene there is a maike;
　　That neither has flesh, nor blood, nor bane;
And down in yon greenwood he walks his lane.

In that green wene Kilmeny lay,
　　Her bosom hap'd wi' flowerets gay;
But the air was soft, and the silence deep,
　　And bonnie Kilmeny fell sound asleep,
She kenned nae mair, nor open'd her e'e,
　　Till wak'd by the hymns of a far countrye.

She woke on a couch of silk sae slim,
　　All stiped wi' the bars of the rainbow's rim;
And lovely beings round were rife,
　　Who erst had travelled mortal life;

31

And aye they smiled and gan' to speer,
  "What spirit has brought this mortal here?"

They clasped her waist, and her hands sae fair,
  They kissed her cheeks, and they kemed her hair;
And round came many a blooming fere,
  Saying, "Bonny Kilmeny, ye're welcome here!"
Women are freed of the littand scorn,
  O blessed be the day Kilmeny was born!
Now shall the lands of spirits see,
  Now shall it ken what a woman may be!

"O bonnie Kilmeny! free frae stain,
  If ever you seek the world again,
That world of sin, of sorrow, and fear,
  O tell of the joys that are waiting here;
And tell of the signs you shall shortly see;
  Of the times that are now, and the times that shall be."

They bore her far to a mountain green,
  To see what mortal never had seen;
And they seated her high on a purple sward,
  And bade her heed what she saw and heard,
And note the changes the spirits wrought;
  For now she lived in the land of thought.
She  looked, and she saw nor sun nor skies,
  But a crystal dome of a thousand dyes;
She looked, and she saw nae land aright,
  But an endless whirl of glory and light:
And radient beings went and came,
  Far swifter than wind, or the linkèd flame.
She hid her e'en frae the dazzling view;
  She looked again, and the scene was new.

Then Kilmeny begged again to see
  The friends she had left in her ain countrye
To tell of the place where she had been,
  And the glories that lay in the land unseen;

To warn the living maidens fair,
The loved of heaven, the spirits' care,
That all whose minds unmeled remain
Shall bloom in beauty when time is gane.

With distant music, soft and deep,
They lulled Kilmeny sound asleep;
And when she awakened, she lay her lane,
All happed with flowers, in the greenwood wene,
When seven long years had come and fled,
When grief was calm and hope was dead,
When scarce was remembered Kilmeny's name,
Late, late in a gloamin' Kilmeny came hame.

But wherever her peaceful form appeared,
The wild beasts of the hill were cheered;
The wolf played blythely round the field,
The lordly byson lowed, and kneeled;
The dun deer wooed with manner bland,
And cowered beneath her lily hand,
And when at eve the woodlands rung,
When hymns of other worlds she sung
In ecstasy of sweet devotion,
O, then the glen was all in motion!
The wild beasts of the forest came,
Broke from their boughts and faulds the tame,
And goved around, charmed and amazed;
Even the dull cattle crooned and gazed,
And murmered, and looked with anxious pain
For something the mystery to explain.
The buzzard came with the throstle-cock;
The corby left her houf in the rock;

The blackbird alang wi' the eagle flew;
The hind came tripping o'er the dew;
The wolf and the kid their raike began,
And the kid and the lamb and the leveret ran;

The hawk and the hern attour them hung,
    And the merle and the mavis forhooyed their young;
And all in a peaceful ring were hurled
    It was like an eve in a sinless world!

When a month and a day had come and gane,
    Kilmeny sought the greenwood wene;
There laid her down on the leaves sae green,
    And Kilmeny on earth was never mair seen.
But O! the words that fell frae her mouth
    Were words of wonder, and words of truth!

But all the land were in fear and dread,
    For they kendna whether she was living or dead.
It wasna her hame, and she couldna remain;
    She left this world of sorrow and pain,
And returned to the land of thought again.

# THE AUTHOR'S ADDRESS
## TO HIS AULD DOG HECTOR

*James Hogg*

Come, my auld, towzy, trusty friend,
    What gars ye look sae dung wi' wae?
D'ye think my favour's at an end,
    Because thy head is turning grey?

Although thy strength begins to fail,
    Its best was spent in serving me;
An' can I grudge thy wee bit meal,
    Some comfort in thy age to gie?

For mony a day, frae sun to sun,
    We've toiled fu' hard wi' ane anither;
An' mony a thousand mile thou'st run,
    To keep my thraward flocks thegither.

To nae thrawn boy nor naughty wife
    Shall thy auld banes become a drudge;
At cats an' callants a' thy life.
    Thou ever bor'st a mortal grudge;

An' whiles thy surly look declared,
    Thou lo'ed the women warst of a';
Because my love wi' thee they shared
    A matter out o' right or law.

When sittin' wi' my bonnie Meg,
    Mair happy than a prince could be,
Thou placed thee by her other leg,
    An' watched her wi' a jealous e'e.

O'er past imprudence, oft alane
    I've shed the saut an' silent tear;
Then sharin' a' my grief an' pain,
    My poor auld friend came snoovin' near.

For a' the days we've sojourned here,
    An' they've been neither fine nor few,
That thought possest thee year to year,
    That a' my griefs arase frae you.

Wi' waesome face an' hingin' head,
    Thou wad'st hae pressed thee to my knee;
While I thy looks as weel could read,
    As thou had'st said in words to me:

"O my dear master, dinna greet;
    What hae I ever done to vex thee?
See here I'm cowrin' at your feet;
    Just take my life if I perplex thee.

"For a' my toil, my wee drap meat
    Is a' the wage I ask of thee;
For whilk I'm oft obliged to wait
    Wi' hungry wame an' patient e'e.

"Whatever wayward course ye steer;
    Whatever sad mischance o'ertake ye;
Man, here is ane will hald ye dear!
    Man, here is ane will ne'er forsake ye!"

An' should grim death thy noddle save
    Till he has made an end o' me,
Ye'll lie a wee while on the grave
    O' ane wha aye was kind to thee.

# LINES TO SIR WALTER SCOTT

*James Hogg*

Sound, my old harp, thy boldest key
To strain of high festivity!
Can'st thou be silent in the brake,
Loitering by Altrive's mountain lake,
When he who gave the hand its sway
That now has tuned thee many a day,
Has gained thee honours trulier won,
Than e'er by sword of Albyn's son;
High guerdon of a soul refined,
The meed of an exalted mind?

Well suits such wreath thy loyal head,
My counsellor, and friend indeed.
Though hard through life I've pressed my way
For many a chill and joyless day,
Since I have lived entrapt to hail
My sovereign's worth, my friend's avail,
And see, what more I prize than gain,
Our forest harp the bays obtain,
I'll ween I have not lived in vain.

Ah! could I dream when first we met,
When by the scanty ingle set,
Beyond the moors where curlews wheel
In Ettrick's bleakest, lonliest shiel,
Conning old songs of other times,
Most uncooth chants and crabbed rhymes —
Could I e'er dream that wayward wight,
Of roguish joke and heart so light,
In whose oft-changing eye I gazed,
Not without dread the head was crazed,
Should e'er, by genius' force alone,
Skim o'er an ocean sailed by none;

All the hid shoals of envy miss,
And gain such noble port as this!

Blessed be the act of sovereign grace,
That raised thee 'bove the rhyming race;
Blessed be the heart and head elate,
The noble generous estimate
That marked thy worth, and owned the hand
Resistless in its native land.
Bootless the waste of empty words,
The pen is worth ten thousand swords.

Long brook thy honours, gallant knight,
So firm of soul, so stanch of right;
For had thy form but reached its prime,
Free from mischance in early time,
No stouter sturdier arm of weir
Had weilded sword or battle spear.
For war thy boardly frame was born,
For battle shout and bugle-horn;
Thy boyish feats, thy youthful dream —
How thy muse kindles at the theme!
Chance marred the path, or Heaven's decree;
How blessed for Scotland and for me!

Scarce sound thy name as't did before,
Walter the Abbot now no more:
Well — let it be — I'll not repine,
But love the title since 'tis thine.
Long brook thy honours, firm to stand
As Eildon rock; and that thy land,
The first e'er won by dint of rhyme,
May bear thy name till latest time,
And stretch from bourn of Abbot's-lea
To Philhope cross, and Eildon Tree,
Is the heart's wish of one who's still
Thy grateful shepherd of the hill!

# THE SKYLARK

*James Hogg*

Bird of the wilderness,
Blithesome and cumberless,
Sweet be thy matin o'er moorland and lea!
Emblem of happiness,
Blest is thy dwelling-place —
Oh, to abide in the desert with thee!

Wild is thy lay and loud,
Far in the downy cloud,
Love gives it energy, love gave it birth.
Where, on thy dewy wing,
Where art thou journeying?
Thy lay is in heaven, thy love is on earth.

O'er fell and fountain sheen,
O'er moor and mountain green,
O'er the red streamer that heralds the day,
Over the cloudlet dim,
Over the rainbow's rim,
Musical cherub, soar, singing, away!

Then, when the gloaming comes,
Low in the heather blooms
Sweet will thy welcome and bed of love be!
Emblem of happiness,
Blest is thy dwelling-place —
Oh, to abide in the desert with thee!

# LOCK THE DOOR, LARISTON

*James Hogg*

"Lock the door, Lariston, lion of Liddesdale;
Lock the door, Lariston, Lowther comes on;
 The Armstrongs are flying,
 The widows are crying,
The Castletown's burning, and Oliver's gone!

"Lock the door, Lariston — high on the weather-gleam
See how the Saxon plumes bob on the sky —
 Yeomen and carbineer,
 Billman and halberdier,
Fierce is the foray, and far is the cry!

"Bewcastle brandishes high his broad scimitar;
Ridley is riding his fleet-footed grey;
 Hidley and Howard there,
 Wandale and Windermere;
Lock the door, Lariston; hold them at bay.

"Why dost thou smile, noble Elliot of Lariston?
Why does the joy-candle gleam in thine eye?
 Thou bold Border ranger
 Beware of thy danger:
Thy foes are relentless, determined, and nigh."

Jack Elliot raised up his steel bonnet and lookit,
His hand grasp'd the sword with a nervous embrace;
 "Ah, welcome, brave foemen,
 On earth there are no men
More gallant to meet in the foray or chase!

"Little know you of the hearts I have hidden here;
Little know you of our moss-troopers' might —
 Linhope and Sorbie true,
 Sundhope and Milburn too,
Gentle in manner, but lions in fight!

"I have Mangerton, Ogilvie, Raeburn, and Netherbie,
Old Sim of Whitram, and all his array;
        Come all Northumberland,
        Teesdale and Cumberland,
Here at the Breaken tower end shall the fray!"

Scowled the broad sun o'er the links of green Liddesdale,
Red as the beacon-light tipped he the wold,
        Many a bold martial eye
        Mirror'd that morning sky,
Never more oped on his orbit of gold.

Shrill was the bugle's note, dreadful the warrior's shout,
Lances and halberds in splinters were borne;
        Helmet and hauberk then
        Braved the claymore in vain,
Buckler and armlet in shivers were shorn.

See how they wane — the proud files of the Windermere!
Howard! ah, woe to thy hopes of the day!
        Hear the wide welkin rend,
        While the Scots' shouts ascend —
"Elliot of Lariston, Elliot for aye!"

# FAREWELL TO ETTRICK

*James Hogg*

Fareweel, green Ettrick, fare-thee-weel!
  I own I'm unco laith to leave thee;
Nane kens the half o' what I feel,
  Nor half the cause I hae to grieve me.

There first I saw the rising morn;
  There first my infant mind unfurled,
To ween that spot where I was born,
  The very centre of the world.

I thought the hills were sharp as knives,
  An' the braid lift lay whomel'd on them,
An' glowred wi' wonder at the wives
  That spak o' ither hill ayon' them.

As ilka year gae something new,
  Addition to my mind or stature,
So fast my love for Ettrick grew,
  Implanted in my very nature.

I had a thought, — a poor vain thought!
  That sometime I might do her honour;
But a' my hopes are come to nought,
  I'm forced to turn my back upon her.

But fare-ye-weel, my native stream,
  Frae a' regret be ye preserved!
Ye'll maybe cherish some at hame,
  Wha dinna jist sae weel deserve't.

Fareweel, my Ettrick, fare-thee-weel!
  I own I'm unco laith to leave thee;
Nane kens the half o' what I feel,
  Nor half o' that I hae to grieve me.

My parents crazy grown wi' eild,
    How I rejoice to stand their stay!
I thought to be their help and shield,
    And comfort till their hindmost day:

Wi' gentle hand to close their een,
    An' weet the yird wi' mony a tear,
That held the dust o' ilka frien';
    O' friends sae tender and sincere;

It winna do; — I maun away
    To yon rough isle, sae bleak an' dun;
Lang will they mourn, baith night an' day
    The absence o' their darling son.

If I should sleep nae mair to wake,
    In yon far isle beyond the tide,
Set up a headstane for my sake,
    An' prent upon its ample side:

"In memory of a shepherd boy,
    Who left us for a distant shore;
Love was his life, and song his joy;
    But now he's dead — we add no more!"

Fareweel, green Ettrick, fare-thee-weel!
    I own I'm something wae to leave thee;
Nane kens the half o' what I feel,
    Nor half the cause I hae to grieve me!

43

# SIR WALTER SCOTT (1771–1832)

*Born in Edinburgh on August 15th, 1771, a weakly child struck down with a paralysis of the leg, Walter Scott's life was early despaired of. He was taken to the country, to Sandy Knowe near Kelso, where kindly grandparents nurtured and cared for him and there was good food and fresh air. Between the ages of three and eight he grew strong in the shadow of Smailholm Tower and was cradled in the stories of Border exploit and romantic poetry. These formative years had an abiding effect on the whole of his later life.*

*Educated at the Royal High School and University in Edinburgh, Scott afterwards followed in his father's footsteps as a solicitor. He was called to the Bar at the age of twenty-one, and was appointed Sheriff of Selkirkshire at twenty-eight. This was home country for Scott. He had Border reiving blood in his veins from Wat o' Harden on his father's side, and the scholarly Rutherford, the Yarrow Cleric, on his mother's.*

*His first home in the Borders was Ashestiel, a lovely old house on the River Tweed between Selkirk and Walkerburn. It was there that Scott continued to put down the foundations for a life of writing. Those were happy days with his devoted wife Charlotte and his children, fishing, hunting, riding and writing in a carefree atmosphere.*

*Abbotsford was acquired in 1812 and the whole family migrated down the valley, with a great cavalcade of cows, chickens, horses, suits of armour and fishing rods. Work was not completed on the now historic home until 1824, by which time the Sheriff was accumulating vast debts — somewhere in the region of £130,000. The publishing and printing firms of Constable and Ballantyne, with whom Scott was deeply involved, were now in ruins. In a great effort to clear his name and to redeem his honour and that of his incompetent business associates, he produced some forty volumes,* Napoleon *alone bringing in £30,000. All this was at a time when ill health was his constant companion, the very effort draining away his life-blood.*

*In his lifetime Scott was feted and honoured by kings and potentates — indeed, he received his baronetcy from the very hand of George IV — yet he ever remained the humble friend of his coachman, Mathieson, and Purdie, his "man". A great lover of horses and dogs, he was keen on a day at the fishing and fond of a night at Tibbie Shiel's in company of Hogg, North and other literary giants of his day.*

*As a measure of public love and devotion to the man who wrote the Waverley Novels and a host of other exciting works — not to mention instigating the rediscovery of the Scottish Regalia in Edinburgh Castle — a monument was raised in Princes Street, Edinburgh which in every way is a majestic memorial to this Wizard of the North, the beloved Shirra of Selkirkshire, the true child of genius.*

*Sir Walter Scott died at his home, Abbotsford, at the age of sixty-one, on Sepember 21st, 1832, and was buried in Dryburgh Abbey. Much has been written about him, but read the man himself and walk or ride with him through the land from Flodden to dark Loch Skene and listen to the singing of his Minstrel or the stentorian bellow of his Marmion echoing down through the years.*

# BORDER MARCH

### From *THE MONASTERY*

### *Sir Walter Scott*

March, march, Ettrick and Teviotdale,
   Why the deil dinna ye march forward in order?
March, march, Eskdale and Liddesdale,
   All the Blue Bonnets are bound for the Border.
     Many a banner spread,
     Flutters above your head,
   Many a crest that is famous in story.
     Mount and make ready then,
     Sons of the mountain glen,
   Fight for the Queen and our old Scottish glory.

Come from the hills where your hirsels are grazing,
   Come from the glen of the buck and the roe;
Come to the crag where the beacon is blazing,
   Come with the buckler, the lance, and the bow.
     Trumpets are sounding
     War-steeds are bounding,
   Stand to your arms, and march in good order,
     England shall many a day
     Tell of the bloody fray,
   When the Blue Bonnets came over the Border.

# ON ETTRICK FOREST'S MOUNTAINS DUN

*Sir Walter Scott*

On Ettrick Forest's mountains dun,
   'Tis blithe to hear the sportsman's gun,
And seek the heath-frequenting brood
   Far through the noon-day solitude;
By many a cairn and trenched mound.
   Where chiefs of yore sleep lone and sound,
And springs, where grey-hair'd shepherds tell,
   That still the fairies love to dwell.

Along the silver streams of Tweed,
   'Tis blithe the mimic fly to lead,
When to hook the salmon springs,
   And the line whistles through the rings;
The boiling eddy see him try,
   Then dashing from the current high,
Till watchful eye and cautious hand
   Have led his wasted strength to land.

'Tis blithe along the midnight tide,
   With stalwart arm the boat to guide;
On high the dazzling blaze to rear,
   And heedful plunge the barbed spear;
Rock, wood and scaur, emerging bright,
   Fling on the stream their ruddy light,
And from the bank our band appears
   Like Genii, arm'd with fiery spears.

'Tis blithe at eve to tell the tale,
   How we succeed, and how we fail,
Whether at Alwyn's lordly meal,
   Or lowlier board of Ashestiel;
While the gay tapers cheerly shine,
   Bickers the fire, and flows the wine —
Days free from thought, and nights from care,
   My blessing on the Forest fair!

# THOMAS THE RHYMER

*Sir Walter Scott*

True Thomas lay on Huntlie bank;
    A ferlie he spied wi' his ee;
And there he saw a ladye bright,
    Come riding down by the Eildon Tree.

Her shirt was o' the grass green silk,
    Her mantle o' the velvet fyne;
At ilka tett of her horse's mane,
    Hung fifty siller bells and nine.

True Thomas, he pull'd aff his cap,
    And louted low down to his knee,
"All hail, thou mighty Queen of Heaven!
    For thy peer on earth I never did see" —

"O no, O no, Thomas, " she said,
    "That name does not belang to me;
I am but the Queen of fair Elfland,
    That am hither come to visit thee.

"Harp and carp, Thomas," she said;
    "Harp and carp along wi' me;
And if ye dare to kiss my lips,
    Sure of your bodie I will be." —

"Betide me weal, betide me woe,
    That weird shall never daunton me." —
Syne he has kiss'd her rosy lips,
    All underneath the Eildon Tree.

"Now, ye maun go wi' me," she said;
    "True Thomas, ye maun go wi' me;
And ye maun serve me seven years,
    Thro' weal or woe as may chance to be."

She mounted on her milk-white steed;
  She's ta'en true Thomas up behind:
Ane aye whene'er her bridle rung,
  The steed flew swifter than the wind.

O they rade on, and farther on;
  The steed gaed swifter than the wind;
Until they reach'd a desert wide,
  And living land was left behind.

"Light down, light down now, true Thomas,
  And lean your head upon my knee;
Abide and rest a little space,
  And I will show you ferlies three.

"O see ye not yon narrow road,
  So thick beset with thorns and briers?
That is the path of righteousness,
  Though after it but few enquires.

"And see not ye that braid braid road,
  That lies across that lily leven?
That is the path of wickedness,
  Though some call it the road to heaven.

"And see not ye that bonny road,
  That winds about the fernie brae?
That is the road to fair Elfland,
  Where thou and I this night maun gae.

"But Thomas, ye maun hold your tongue,
  Whatever ye may hear or see;
For, if ye speak word in Elflyn land,
  Ye'll ne'er get back to your ain countrie."

O they rade on, and farther on,
  And they waded through rivers aboon the knee,
And they saw neither sun nor moon,
  But they heard the roaring of the sea.

It was mirk mirk night, and there was nae stern light,
   And they waded through red blude to the knee,
For a' the blude that's shed on earth
   Rins through the springs o' that countrie.

Syne they came on to a garden green,
   And she pu'd an apple frae a tree —
"Take this for thy wages, true Thomas;
   It will give thee the tongue that can never lie." —

"My tongue is mine ain," true Thomas said;
   "A gudely gift ye wad gie to me!
I neither dought to buy nor sell,
   At fair or tryst where I may be.

"I dought neither speak to prince or peer,
   Nor ask of grace from fair ladye." —
"Now hold thy peace!" the lady said,
   "For as I say, so must it be." —

He has gotten a coat of the even cloth,
   And a pair of shoes of velvet green;
And till seven years were gane and past,
   True Thomas on earth was never seen.

# MARMION

## *Sir Walter Scott*

## *LOCHINVAR*

O, young Lochinvar is come out of the west,
Through all the wide Border his steed was the best;
And save his good broadsword, he weapons had none,
He rode all unarm'd, and he rode all alone,
So faithful in love and so dauntless in war,
There never was knight like the young Lochinvar.

He staid not for brake, and he stopp'd not for stone,
He swam the Esk river where ford there was none;
But ere he alighted at Netherby gate,
The bride had consented, the gallant came late:
For a laggard in love, and a dastard in war,
Was to wed the fair Ellen of brave Lochinvar.

So boldly he enter'd the Netherby Hall,
Among bride's-men, and kinsmen, and brothers, and all:
Then spoke the bride's father, his hand on his sword
(For the poor craven bridegroom said never a word),
"O come ye in peace here, or come ye in war,
Or to dance at our bridal, young Lord Lochinvar?" —

"I long woo'd your daughter, my suit you denied; —
Love swells like the Solway, but ebbs like its tide —
And now I am come, with this lost love of mine,
To lead but one measure, drink one cup of wine.
There are maidens in Scotland more lovely by far,
That would gladly be bride to the young Lochinvar."

The bride kiss'd the goblet: the knight took it up,
He quaff'd off the wine, and he threw down the cup.
She look'd down to blush, and she look'd up to sigh,
With a smile on her lips, and a tear in her eye.

He took her soft hand, ere her mother could bar, —
"Now tread we a measure!" said young Lochinvar.

So stately his form and so lovely her face,
That never a hall such a galliard did grace;
While her mother did fret, and her father did fume,
And the bridegroom stood dangling his bonnet and plume;
And the bride-maidens whisper'd " 'Twere better by far,
To have match'd our fair cousin with young Lochinvar."

One touch to her hand, and one word in her ear,
When they reach'd the hall-door, and the charger stood near;
So light to the croupe the fair lady he swung,
So light to the saddle before her he sprung!
"She is won! we are gone, over bank, bush, and scaur;
They'll have fleet steeds that follow," quoth young Lochinvar.

There was mounting 'mong Graemes of the Netherby clan;
Forsters, Fenwicks, and Musgraves, they rode and they ran:
There was racing and chasing on Cannonbie Lee,
But the lost bride of Netherby ne'er did they see.
So daring in love, and so dauntless in war,
Have you e'er heard of gallant like young Lochinvar?

# THE LAY OF THE LAST MINSTREL

*Sir Walter Scott*

## INTRODUCTION

The way was long, the wind was cold,
    The Minstrel was infirm and old;
His wither'd cheek, and tresses grey,
    Seem'd to have known a better day;
The harp, his sole remaining joy,
    Was carried by an orphan boy.
The last of all the Bards was he,
    Who sung of Border chivalry;
For, welladay! their date was fled,
    His tuneful brethren all were dead;
And he, neglected and oppress'd,
    Wish'd to be with them, and at rest.
No more on prancing palfrey borne,
    He caroll'd light as lark at morn;
No longer courted and caress'd,
    High placed in hall, a welcome guest,
He pour'd to lord and lady gay,
    The unpremeditated lay:
Old times were changed, old manners gone,
    A stranger fill'd the Stuarts' throne;
The bigots of the iron time
    Had call'd his harmless art a crime.
A wandering Harper, scorn'd and poor,
    He begg'd his bread from door to door,
And tuned, to please a peasant's ear,
    The harp, a king had loved to hear.

He pass'd where Newark's stately tower
    Looks out from Yarrow's birchen bower:
The Minstrel gazed with wishful eye —
    No humbler resting-place was nigh.

With hesitating step at last,
   The embattled portal arch he pass'd
Whose ponderous grate and massy bar
   Had oft roll'd back the tide of war,
But never closed the iron door
   Against the desolate and poor.
The Duchess mark'd his weary pace,
   His timid mien, and reverend face,
And bade her page the menials tell,
   That they should tend the old man well;
For she had known adversity,
   Though born in such a high degree;
In pride of power, in beauty's bloom,
   Had wept o'er Monmouth's bloody tomb.

When kindness had his wants supplied,
   And the old man was gratified,
Began to rise his minstrel pride:
   And he began to talk anon,
In varying cadence, soft or strong,
   He swept the sounding chords along:
The present scene, the future lot,
   His toils, his wants, were all forgot:
Cold diffidence, and age's frost,
   In the full tide of song were lost;
Each blank, in faithless memory void,
   The poet's glowing thought supplied;
And, while his harp responsive rung,
   'Twas thus the LATEST MINSTREL sung.

## MELROSE

If thou wouldst view fair Melrose aright,
   Go visit it by the pale moonlight;
For the gay beams of lightsome day
   Gild, but to flout, the ruins grey.
When the broken arches are black in night,

And each shafted oriel glimmers white;
When the cold light's uncertain shower
    Streams on the ruin'd central tower;
When buttress and buttress, alternately,
    Seem framed of ebon and ivory;
When silver edges the imagery,
    And the scrolls that teach thee to live and die;
When distant Tweed is heard to rave.
    And the owlet to hoot o'er the dead man's grave,
Then go — but go alone the while —
    Then view St David's ruin'd pile;
And home returning, soothly swear,
    Was never scene so sad and fair!

## THE WIZARD

They sat them down on a marble stone
    (A Scottish monarch slept below;)
    Thus spoke the monk, in solemn tone:—
"I was not always a man of woe;
    For Paynim countries I have trod,
And fought beneath the Cross of God:
    Now, strange to my eyes thine arms appear,
And their iron clang sounds strange to my ear".
    "In these far climes it was my lot
To meet the wondrous Michael Scott,
    A wizard of such dreaded fame,
That when, in Salamanca's cave,
    Him listed his magic wand to wave,
The bells would ring in Notre Dame!
    Some of his skill he taught to me;
And, Warrior, I could say to thee
    The words that cleft Eildon hills in three,
And bridled the Tweed with a curb of stone:
    But to speak them were a deadly sin;
And for having but thought them my heart within,
    A treble penance must be done.

55

"When Michael lay on his dying bed,
    His conscience was awakened:
He bethought him of his sinful deed,
    And he gave me a sign to come with speed:
I was in Spain when the morning rose,
    But I stood by his bed ere evening close,
The words may not again be said,
    That he spoke to me, on death-bed laid;
They would rend this Abbayes's massy nave,
    And pile it in heaps above his grave.

"I swore to bury his Mighty Book,
    That never mortal might therein look;
And never to tell where it was hid,
    Save at his Chief of Branksome's need:
And when that need was past and o'er,
    Again the volume to restore.
I buried him on St Michael's night,
    When the bell toll'd one, and the moon was bright,
And I dug his chamber among the dead,
    When the floor of the chancel was stained red,
That his patron's cross might over him wave,
    And scare the fiends from the Wizard's grave.

Slow moved the monk to the broad flag-stone,
    Which the bloody Cross was traced upon:
He pointed to a secret nook;
    An iron bar the Warrior took;
And the monk made a sign with his wither'd hand,
    The grave's huge portal to expand.
With beating heart to the task he went;
    His sinewy frame o'er the grave-stone bent;
With bar of iron heaved amain,
    Till the toil-drops fell from his brows, like rain.
It was by dint of passing strength,
    That he moved the massy stone at length.
I would you had been there, to see

How the light broke forth so gloriously,
Stream'd upward to the chancel roof,
And through the galleries far aloof!
No earthly flame blazed e'er so bright:
It shone like heaven's own blessed light,
And, issuing from the tomb,
Show'd the Monk's cowl, and visage pale,
Danced on the dark-brow'd Warrior's mail
And kiss'd his waving plume.

Before their eyes the Wizard lay,
As if he had not been dead a day.
His hoary beard in silver roll'd
He seem'd some seventy winters old;
A palmer's amice wrapp'd him round,
With a wrought Spanish baldric bound,
Like a pilgrim from beyond the sea:
His left hand held his Book of Might;
A silver cross was in his right;
The lamp was placed beside his knee:
High and majestic was his look,
At which the fellest fiends had shook,
And all unruffled was his face:
They trusted his soul had gotten grace.

Often had William of Deloraine
Rode through the battle's bloody plain,
And trampled down the warriors slain,
And neither known remorse nor awe;
Yet now remorse and awe he own'd,
His breath came thick, his head swam round,
When this strange scene of death he saw.
Bewilder'd and unnerv'd he stood,
And the priest pray'd fervently and loud:
With eyes averted prayed he;
He might not endure the sight to see.
Of the man he had loved so brotherly.

And when the priest his death-prayer had pray'd,
  Thus unto Deloraine he said:—
Now, speed thee what thou hast to do,
  Or, Warrior we may dearly rue;
For those, thou mayst not look upon,
  Are gathering fast round the yawning stone!" —
Then Deloraine, in terror, took
  From the cold hand the Mighty Book,
With iron clasp'd, and with iron bound:
  He thought, as he took it, the dead man frown'd;
But the glare of the sepulchral light,
  Perchance, had dazzled the warrior's sight.
When the huge stone sunk o'er the tomb,
  The night return'd in double gloom.


### INTERLUDE

Alas! fair dames, your hopes are vain!
  My harp has lost the enchanting strain;
Its lightness would my age reprove:
  My hairs are grey, my limbs are old,
My heart is dead, my veins are cold:
  I may not, must not, sing of love.
Full slyly smiled the observant page,
  And gave the wither'd hand of age
A goblet crown'd with mighty wine,
  The blood of Velez scorched vine.
He raised the silver cup on high,
  And, while the big drop fill'd his eye,
Pray'd God to bless the Duchess long,
  And all who cheer'd a son of song.
The attending maidens smiled to see
  How long, how deep, how zealously,
The precious juice the Minstrel quaff'd
  And he, embolden'd by the draught,
Look'd gaily back to them, and laugh'd.

The cordial nectar of the bowl
Swell'd his old veins, and cheer'd his soul;
   A lighter, livelier prelude ran,
Ere thus this tale again began.


## AULD WAT

An aged Knight, to danger steel'd
   With many a moss-trooper, came on;
And azure in a golden field,
   The stars and crescent graced his shield,
Without the bend of Murdieston.
   Wide lay his lands round Oakwood tower,
And wide round haunted Castle-Ower;
   High over Borthwick's mountain flood,
His wood embosom'd mansion stood;
   In the dark glen, so deep below,
The herds of plunder'd England low;
   His bold retainers' daily food,
And bought with danger, blows, and blood.
   Marauding chief! his sole delight
The moonlight raid, the morning fight;
   Not even the Flower of Yarrow's charms,
In youth, might tame his rage for arms;
   And still, in age he spurn'd at rest,
And still his brows the helmet press'd,
   Albeit the blanched locks below
Were white as Dinlay's spotless snow:
   Five stately warriors drew the sword
Before their father's band;
   A braver knight than Harden's lord
Ne'er belted on a brand.

Breathes there the man, with soul so dead,
  Who never to himself hath said,
This is my own, my native land!
  Whose heart hath ne'er within him burn'd,
  As home his footsteps he hath turn'd,
    From wandering on a foreign strand!
If such there breathe, go, mark him well;
    For him no Minstrel raptures swell;
High though his titles, proud his name,
    Boundless his wealth as wish can claim;
Despite those titles, power and pelf,
    The wretch, concentred all in self,
Living, shall forfeit fair renown,
    And, doubly dying, shall go down
To the vile dust, from whence he sprung,
    Unwept, unhonour'd, and unsung.

O Caledonia! stern and wild,
    Meet nurse for a poetic child!
Land of brown heath and shaggy wood,
    Land of the mountain and the flood,
Land of my sires! what mortal hand
    Can e'er untie the filial band,
That knits me to thy rugged strand!
    Still, as I view each well-known scene,
Think what is now, and what hath been,
    Seems as, to me, of all bereft,
Sole friends thy woods and streams were left;
    And thus I love them better still,
Even in extremity of ill.
    By Yarrow's streams still let me stray,
Though none should guide my feeble way;
    Still feel the breeze down Ettrick break,
Although it chill my wither'd cheek;
    Still lay my head by Teviot Stone,

Though there, forgotten and alone,
  The bard may draw his parting groan.

Hush'd is the harp — the Minstrel gone.
  And did he wander forth alone?
Alone, in indigence and age,
  To linger out his pilgrimage?
No! — close beneath proud Newark's tower
  Arose the Minstrel's lowly bower;
A simple hut; but there was seen
  The little garden hedged with green,
The cheerful hearth, and lattice clean.
  There shelter'd wanderers, by the blaze,
Oft heard the tale of other days;
  For much he loved to ope his door,
And give the aid he begg'd before.
  So pass'd the winter's day; but still,
When summer smiled on sweet Bowhill,
  And July's eve, with balmy breath,
Waved the blue-bells on Newark heath;
  When throstles sung in Harehead-shaw,
And corn was green on Carterhaugh,
  And flourish'd, broad, Blackandro's oak,
The aged Harper's soul awoke!
  Then would he sing achievements high,
And circumstance of chivalry,
  Till the rapt traveller would stay,
Forgetful of the closing day;
  And noble youths, the strain to hear,
Forsook the hunting of the deer;
  And Yarrow, as he roll'd along,
Bore burden to the Minstrel's song.

# WILLIAM LAIDLAW (1780–1845)

*Born on November 19th, 1780, at the farm of Blackhouse on the Douglas Burn and near to St Mary's Loch, William was the eldest of three sons. The father, James Laidlaw, was an extremely able and intelligent man, and a good farmer. James Hogg came to be shepherd at the Laidlaw farmstead when Willie was ten years old and receiving his education at Peebles Grammar School. Jamie and Willie became firm friends and when Scott and Leyden came visiting and looking for material for the Minstrelsy, a small literary society was in the making. When Willie produced a copy of "Auld Maitland" Scott was greatly taken with it and recited it out loud, developing that distinctive "burr" that came into his voice when excited.*

*The bond of friendship which was formed at that time remained constant to the end of their days. When Willie didn't succeed too well at farming, Scott made him factor at Abbotsford, where he also acted as secretary to Sir Walter and was his constant companion. When Scott died in 1832 Willie moved to Ross-shire and factored there for a while, and later moved to Contin near Dingwall where he died at the age of sixty-five on May 18th, 1845.*

*The beautiful poem "Lucy's Flittin' "is Laidlaw's lasting memorial. He wrote other works and songs: "Her Bonnie Black E'e" is but one of them. He also wrote on geological affairs in the county and made contributions to literary magazines.*

# LUCY'S FLITTIN'

*William Laidlaw*

'Twas when the wan leaf frae the birk tree was fa'in',
   And Martinmas dowie had wound up the year,
That Lucy row'd up her wee kist, wi' her a' in,
   And left her auld master and neebours sae dear,
For Lucy had served i' the glen a' the simmer;
   She cam' there afore the flow'r bloom'd on the pea;
An orphan was she, an' they had been gude till her,
   Sure that was the thing brocht the tear in her e'e.

She gaed by the stable where Jamie was stan'in';
   Richt sair was his kind heart the flittin' to see.
"Fare ye weel, Lucy," quo Jamie, and ran in,
   The gatherin' tears trickled fast frae his e'e.
As doun the burnside she gaed slow wi' her flittin',
   "Fare ye weel, Lucy," was ilka bird's sang.
She heard the craw sayin't, high on the tree sittin',
   And Robin was chirpin't the brown leaves amang.

"Oh! what is't that pits my puir heart in a flutter?
   An' what gars the tear come sae fast to my e'e?
If I wasna ettled to be ony better,
   Then what gars me wish ony better to be?
I'm just like a lammie that loses its mither;
   Nae mither or friend the puir lammie can see;
I fear I hae left my bit heart a' thegither,
   Nae wonder the tear fa's sae fast frae my e'e.

"Wi' the rest o' my claes I hae row'd up the ribbon,
   The bonny blue ribbon that Jamie ga'e me;
Yestreen, when he ga'e me't and saw I was sabbin',
   I'll never forget the wae blink o' his e'e.
Though now he said naething but 'Fare ye weel, Lucy!'
   It made me I neither could speak, hear nor see;

He couldna say mair, but just 'Fare ye weel, Lucy!'
  Yet that I will mind till the day that I dee.

"The lamb likes the gowan wi' dew when its droukit;
  The hare likes the brake, and the braird on the lee;
But Lucie likes Jamie;" — she turned and she lookit,
  She thocht the dear place she wad never mair see.
Ah! weel may young Jamie·gang dowie and cheerless!
  And weel may he greet on the bank o' the burn!
For bonny sweet Lucy sae gentle an' peerless,
  Lies cauld in her grave, and will never return.

*Scott's last resting-
place —
Dryburgh Abbey*

# DR JOHN LEYDEN (1775–1811)

## POET AND LINGUIST

*John Leyden was born on September 8th, 1775, the son of a humble shepherd living in a thatched cottage by the side of Denholm Green. The village is situated on the south side of the River Teviot, about four miles from the Border town of Hawick. The young lad's father and grandmother first taught him to read and, like so many of his contemporaries, his text book was the Bible; then he was slowly weaned on tales of Bruce and Wallace: he could recite the ballads of the day, and learned a healthy fear of demons and goblins.*

*The family moved to the farm of Henslawshill near Ruberslaw, and there their number increased by another three sons and two daughters. John, from a very early age, showed unusual aptitude; a great uncle took a special interest in him and filled his mind with stories of the past. By the age of ten he was at school at Kirkton where, among other things, he studied Latin and arithmetic. In October 1790 he set off for Edinburgh to study for the Ministry. He rode with his father as far as Galashiels and there took a fond farewell and walked the rest of the way to the big city. His "kist" containing a change of clothing and boots, eggs, cheese, lentils, a bag of oatmeal and potatoes, was sent on by carrier from home. Not many with such a humble background then aspired to University life, but John excelled in everything he put his mind to. He was an excellent Latin and Greek scholar, and also studied French, Spanish, Italian, German, Hebrew, Arabic and Persian, as well as mathematics and science — in addition of course to Divinity and other kindred subjects.*

*When at home in the Borders, Leyden was constantly out in the countryside: he seemed to draw strength from it. He roamed with Scott in search of Border ballads and spent*

*long hours in his company, with Hogg and Willie Laidlaw.
Scott said that they returned from these trips "loaded with
treasures of oral tradition". "The Court of Keeldar",
"Lord Soulis" and "The Mermaid", which appear in the*
Minstrelsy of the Scottish Border, *came from John
Leyden's hand.*

*Leyden was licensed to the Kirk in Edinburgh but he
never actually took up a living, though he did preach and
lecture. He was at a disadvantage in the pulpit as he had
rather a harsh, shrill voice and was not of the most prepos-
sessing appearance. His heart, moreover, seemed set on go-
ing abroad. He had hoped for some appointment connected
with Eastern languages but the only opening which could
be found was for an assistant-surgeon in Madras in India.
Within six months Leyden, who had already been attend-
ing classes in medicine before completing his studies for
the Ministry, successfully qualified himself for this new
profession at St Andrews. This was in 1802, the same year
that he wrote* Scenes of Infancy.

*The following year Leyden left Scotland forever. In
India his appetite for study remained insatiable and, even
when down with a bout of fever, he could put in ten hours
of work a day. In Calcutta he was appointed Professor of
Hindustani; he was also an Assayer and a Judge to the
Supreme Court, where he might need to speak seven differ-
ent languages in a day. Indeed, during his short lifetime he
acquired a command of thirty-four languages, and had
some acquaintance with no less than forty-five!*

*The Governor of British India at this time was Lord
Minto, who, when he discovered Leyden, took a great in-
terest in the brilliant lad from the village of Denholm, which
lay beside the Estate of Minto: Border blood ran thick
though rank was different. In 1811 Leyden sailed with
Lord Minto's Java expedition as a Malay interpreter. When
Batavia was captured he quickly moved into the city to
pore over books in the library, where, it is said, he caught*

a fever when helping to pave the way for a new Government under Lord Minto. He died at the early age of thirty-six.

So ended a short and exciting life. We have in our hands some of the poetry by which to remember this much admired and humble man, who had, as well as great learning, a great sense of fun and good humour. A monument of another sort to his memory stands on Denholm Green; it is made of red granite from Peterhead and freestone from Swinton Quarry.

**Thomas The Rhymer's Tower Earlston**

# SCENES OF INFANCY

*John Leyden*

## THE JED

Dear native valleys! may ye long retain
    The charter'd freedom of the mountain swain!
Long mid your sounding glades, in union sweet,
    May rural innocence and beauty meet!
And still be duly heard, at twilight calm,
    From every cot the peasant's chaunted psalm!
Then, Jedworth! though thy ancient choirs shall fade,
    And time lay bare each lofty colonnade,
From the damp roof the massy sculptures die,
    And in their vaults thy rifted arches lie,
Still in these vales shall angel harps prolong,
    By Jed's pure stream, a sweeter even-song,
Than long processions, once, with mystic zeal,
    Pour'd to the harp and solemn organ's peal.
O softly, Jed! thy sylvan current lead
    Round every hazel copse and smiling mead,
Where lines if firs the glowing landscape screen,
    And crown the heights with tufts of deeper green.

## HILL BIRDS

How wild and harsh the moorland music floats,
    When clamorous curlew scream with long-drawn notes,
Or, faint and piteous, wailing plovers pipe,
    Or, loud and louder still, the soaring snipe!
And here the lonely lapwing whoops along,
    That piercing shrieks her still-repeated song,
Flaps her blue wing, displays her pointed crest,
    And cowering lures the peasant from her nest.

68

But if where all her dappled treasure lies
  He bends his steps, no more she round him flies;
Forlorn, despairing of a mother's skill,
  Silent, and sad, she seeks the distant hill.


## DEATH

Sweet scenes, conjoined with all that most endears
  The cloudless morning of my tender years!
With fond regret your haunts I wander o'er,
  And wondering feel myself the child no more:
Your forms, your sunny tints, are still the same; —
  But sad the tear which lost affections claim.

Aurelia! mark yon silver clouds unroll'd,
  Where far in ether hangs each shining fold,
That on the breezy billow idly sleeps,
  Or climbs ambitious up the azure steeps!
Their snowy ridges seem to heave and swell
  With airy domes, where parted spirits dwell;
Untainted souls, from this terrestrial mould
  Who fled, before the priest their names had told.

On such an eve as this, so mild and clear,
  I follow'd to the grave a sister's bier.
As sad, by Teviot, I retir'd alone,
  The setting sun with silent splendour shone;
Sublime emotions reach'd my purer mind;
  The fear of death, the world was left behind.
I saw the thin-spread clouds of summer lie,
  Like shadows, on the soft cerulean sky:
As each its silver bosom seem'd to bend,
  Rapt fancy heard an angel-voice descend,
Melodious as the strain which floats on high,
  To soothe the sleep of blameless infancy.

## TO HIS SHADOW*

"But when I left my father's old abode,
   And thou the sole companion of my road,
As sad I paused, and fondly looked behind,
   And almost deemed each face I met unkind,
While kindling hopes to boding fears gave place,
   Thou seem'd'st the ancient Spirit of my Race.
In startled Fancy's ear I heard thee say,
   'Ha! I will meet thee after many a day,
When Youth's impatient joys, too fierce to last,
   And Fancy's wild illusions all are past;
Yes! I will come, when scenes of youth depart,
   To ask thee for thy innocence of heart —
To ask thee, when thou bid'st this light adieu,
   Ha! wilt thou blush thy Ancestors to view?' "


## JAMES PURVIS

Purvis, when on this eastern strand,
   With glad surprise I grasp thy hand;
And memory's fancy's powers employ
   In the form'd man to trace the boy:
How many dear illusions rise,
   And scenes long faded from my eyes,
Since first our bounding steps were seen,
   Active and light, on Denholm's level green!

Playmate of boyhood's ardent prime!
   Rememberest thou, in former time,
How oft we bade, in fickle freak,
   Adieu to Latin terms and Greek,

* On leaving home for university in Edinburgh

To trace the banks where blackbirds sung,
  And ripe brown nuts in clusters hung —
Where tangled hazels twined a screen
  Of shadowy boughs in Denholm's mazy Dene?

Rememberest thou, in youthful might,
  Who foremost dared the mimic fight,
And, proud to feel his sinews strung,
  Aloft the knotted cudgel swung;
Or fist to fist, with gore embrued,
  The combat's wrathful strife pursued,
With eager heart, and fury keen,
  Amid the ring on Denholm's bustling green?

## DARK RUBERSLAW

Dark Ruberslaw, that lifts his head sublime,
  Rugged and hoary with the wreaks of time!
On his broad misty front the giant wears
  The horrid furrows of ten thousand years;
His aged brows are crowned with curling fern,
  Where perches, grave and lone, the hooded erne,
Majestic bird! by ancient shepherds styled,
  The lonely hermit of the russet wild,
That loves, amid the stormy blast to soar,
  When through disjointed cliffs the tempests roar,
Climbs on strong wing the storm, and, screaming high,
  Rides the dim rack that sweeps the darkened sky.

71

# WILLIAM WORDSWORTH (1770–1850)

*Born at Cockermouth in Cumberland on April 7th, 1770, the second son of John Wordsworth, attorney and land agent to the Earl of Lonsdale, William first went to school in Penrith and later to Hawkshead School in Lancashire.*

*In the magnificent scenery of his boyhood days, a poetic fire was kindled which was never to go out. It ultimately found fulfilment in "The Daffodils", "The Cuckoo" and a host of nature poems of intense beauty.*

*In the year 1787 he went to Cambridge for four years and took a Bachelor of Arts degree, but did not excel as a scholar. Like most poets he came in for his share of severe criticism in his early writings, but took it all rather philosophically, and prevailed in the end.*

*When visiting Scotland with his sister Dorothy, he came within hailing distance of Yarrow, but never ventured past Clovenfords. He wrote the poem "Yarrow Unvisited" with its longings and hopes of another day. "Yarrow Visited" was written in 1814 when he came to the valley in company with James Hogg, the Ettrick Shepherd. With Sir Walter Scott as his escort, Wordsworth paid a third visit to the valley and called in at Newark Castle, that once magnificent hunting lodge of kings. Scott was dying and Wordsworth could feel it; the sadness seems to pervade his verses in "Yarrow Revisited".*

*William Wordsworth died in 1850 and lies buried in an idyllic resting-place in Grasmere in the Lake District.*

# YARROW VISITED

*William Wordsworth*

And is this — Yarrow? — This the stream
Of which my fancy cherished,
So faithfully, a waking dream?
An image that hath perished!
O that some Minstrel's harp were near,
To utter notes of gladness,
And chase this silence from the air,
That fills my heart with sadness!

Yet why? — a silvery current flows
With uncontrolled meanderings;
Nor have these eyes by greener hills
Been soothed, in all my wanderings.
And, through her depths, Saint Mary's Lake
Is visibly delighted;
For not a feature of those hills
Is in the mirror slighted.

A blue sky bends o'er Yarrow vale,
Save where that pearly whiteness
Is round the rising sun diffused,
A tender hazy brightness;
Mild dawn of promise! that excludes
All profitless dejection;
Though not unwilling here to admit
A pensive recollection. —

Where was it that the famous Flower
Of Yarrow Vale lay bleeding?
His bed per chance was yon smooth mound
On which the herd is feeding:
And haply from this crystal pool,
Now peaceful as the morning,

The Water-wraith ascended thrice —
And gave his doleful warning.

Delicious is the Lay that sings
The haunts of happy Lovers,
The path that leads them to the grove,
The leafy grove that covers:
And Pity sanctifies the verse
That paints, by strength of sorrow,
The unconquerable strength of love;
Bear witness, rueful Yarrow.

But thou, that did'st appear so fair
To fond imagination,
Dost rival in the light of day
Her delicate creation:
Meek loveliness is round thee spread,
A softness still and holy;
The grace of forest charms decayed,
And pastoral melancholy.

That region left, the vale unfolds
Rich groves of lofty stature,
With Yarrow winding through the pomp
Of cultivated nature;
And, rising from those lofty groves,
Behold a Ruin hoary!
The shattered front of Newark's Towers,
Renowned in Border story.

Fair scenes for childhood's opening bloom,
For sportive youth to stray in;
For manhood to enjoy his strength;
And age to wear away in!
Yon cottage seems a bower of bliss,
A covert for protection
Of tender thoughts, that nestle there —
The brood of chaste affection.

How sweet, on this autumnal day,
The wild-wood fruits to gather,
And on my True-love's forehead plant,
A crest of blooming heather!
And what if I enwreathed my own!
'Twere no offence to reason;
The sober hills thus deck their brows
To meet the wintry season.

I see — but not by sight alone,
Loved Yarrow, have I won thee;
A ray of fancy still survives —
Her sunshine plays upon thee!
Thy ever youthful waters keep
A course of lively pleasure;
And gladsome notes my lips can breathe,
Accordant to the measure.

The vapours linger round the Heights,
They melt, and soon must vanish;
One hour is theirs nor more is mine —
Sad thoughts which I would banish,
But that I know where'er I go,
Thy geniune image, Yarrow!
Will dwell with me — to heighten joy,
And cheer my mind in sorrow.

# J. B. SELKIRK (1832–1904)

*A real son of the Borders, his actual name was James B. Brown. He was born in Galashiels in 1832, the year Sir Walter Scott died. Henry Brown, his father, was co-founder of the Ettrick Tweed Mills in Selkirk, and one of the pioneers of the tweed industry in the area. James followed his father as a manufacturer, after receiving his basic education at Selkirk Grammar School and continuing it at the Edinburgh Institute.*

*J. B. Selkirk was a great lover of nature and had an abiding passion for the countryside, and Yarrow in particular. Early in life his pen was busy; poetry flowed easily from him. The music of the Border tongue is kept alive in his work: "Twa muckle e'en" defies translation! "Sittin' chirpin' a' its lane, A water-waggy on a stane," is sweet language indeed to the Border ear. He described our ballads as "Scotland's richest poetical heritage".*

*Ill health dogged his path and at the age of twenty, confined to his room for a whole year, J. B. S. wrote the book* Bible Truths and Shakespearian Parallels, *and later* Ethics and Aesthetics of Modern Poetry. *He was a prolific letter writer and wrote in a beautiful hand. He contributed essays to* Blackwoods *and other periodicals and was very musical, a great lover of Schubert and Beethoven. He was a contemporary of Tom Scott, R.S.A., and was a fair artist himself. He was a sensitive man, easily moved to tears, even by the song of a lintie. A volume of his poems was published in 1911, and it has found a resting place in the hearts of all true Borderers.*

*J. B. Selkirk died on Christmas day in 1904 at the age of seventy-two and was buried in Selkirk. A simple plaque, situated just beside the Flodden Memorial, was unveiled to him in 1931.*

# A SONG OF YARROW

*J. B. Selkirk*

September, and the sun was low,
    The tender greens were flecked with yellow,
And autumn's ardent after-glow
    Made Yarrow's uplands rich and mellow.

Between me and the sunken sun,
    Where gloaming gathered in the meadows,
Contented cattle, red and dun,
    Were slowly browsing in the shadows.

And out beyond them Newark reared
    Its quiet tower against the sky,
As if its walls had never heard
    Of wassail-rout or battle-cry.

O'er moss-grown roofs that once had rung
    To reiver's riot, Border brawl,
The slumberous shadows mutely hung,
    And silence deepened over all.

Above the high horizon bar
    A cloud of golden mist was lying,
And over it a single star
    Soared heavenward as the day was dying.

No sound, no word, from field or ford,
    Nor breath of wind to float a feather,
While Yarrow's murmuring waters poured
    A lonely music through the heather.

In silent fascination bound,
    As if some mighty spell obeying,
The hills stood listening to the sound,
    And wondering what the stream was saying.

What secret to the inner ear,
   What happier message, was it bringing,
With more of hope, and less of fear,
   Than men dare mix with earthly singing?

Earth's song it was, yet heavenly growth —
   It was not joy, it was not sorrow —
A strange heart-fulness of them both
   The wandering singer seemed to borrow.

Like one that sings and does not know,
   But in a dream hears voices calling,
Of those that died long years ago,
   And sings although the tears be falling.

Oh Yarrow! garlanded with rhyme
   That clothes thee in a mournful glory,
Though sunsets of an elder time
   Had never crowned thee with a story, —

Still would I wander by thy stream,
   Still listen to the lonely singing,
That gives me back the golden dream
   Through which old echoes yet are ringing.

Love's sunshine! sorrow's bitter blast!
   Dear Yarrow, we have seen together;
For years have come, and years have past,
   Since first we met among the heather.

Ah! those, indeed, were happy hours
   When first I knew thee, gentle river;
But now thy bonny birken bowers
   To me, alas, are changed for ever!

The best, the dearest, all have gone,
   Gone like the bloom upon the heather,
And left us singing here alone,
   Beside life's cold and winter weather.

I, too, pass on, but when I'm dead
   Thou still shalt sing by night and morrow,
And help the aching heart and head
   To bear the burden of its sorrow.

And summer's flowers shall linger yet
   Where all thy mossy margins guide thee;
And minstrels, met as we have met,
   Shall sit and sing their songs beside thee.

*The bridge
at Ashestiel*

# EPISTLE TO TAMMUS*

### J. B. Selkirk

Dear Tam, last mail the wife wad tell
That I had had a gey bit spell
O' wakish health. It's no' like me,
That a' my life hae aye been free
Frae troubles, and was never kent
To hae a serious complent.
I never tuke to bed but wance,
And that was but an orra chance.
Ye mind o' fishin', you and me —
We had been catchin' twae or three —
Among the rocks ahint Brigend,
When, castin' oot, wi' extra bend
I slippit off a muckle stane,
And brak', ye mind, my collar-bane.
I've never been laid up sin' syne,
Nor yet afor'd, that I can min'.

But this is waur; I'm off the streicht,
Week after week I'm losin' weicht,
Until at last, it stands to raison,
I'm just a thing for hingin' claes on.
We've had a doctor, clever man,
And he's dune a' that doctor can, —
A man respeckit near and fer;
His grannie was a Sprouston Ker.
Ye see I'll no' forsake my order;
Till daith, I'll aye uphaud the Border.
We've some grand specimens oot here,
For still they come, frae year to year.
Ane disna need to hear them talk,
Ye ken them by their very walk.

*A letter from a Border emigrant to his
friend in Ettrick

There's Gibbie Elliot, Kinmont Rob,
Aye rouch and raucle for a job;
They'll sleep as sound ahint a dyke
As row'd in blankets on a tyke.
There's Telfer, Douglas, Learmont, Scott,
And thaim that joined the Ancrum lot.
Wi' siccan names there's little fear
That Border bluid will fail oot here.

The Border? Hoots! I'm off the stot.
Where was I? for I've clean forgot.
I have ye, — I was skin and bone,
It was the doctor we were on.
Weel, every time he cam' alang
He couldna find oot what was wrang,
And yet when he took stock o' me
He didna like the look o' me.
Although nae doot I had a teasick,
It's no', said he, a case for pheesick;
So there the doctor's treatment ends,
But guess ye what he recommends?
"What say ye to a voyage hame?"
Oh, Tam, it set my heart aflame;
And as for answer, I was dumb, —
The word was there, it wadna come.
I fand my senses turnin' dizzy;
I glower'd at him, and then at Lizzie.
Out spak' the doctor, fair and square,
"Gudeman, I can do naething mair.
It's after carefu' keen reveesion
I've come at length to this decision.
I've had some cases like your ain
Where a' my treatment's been in vain.
Wi' lads and lassies naething's wantin',
But auld folk dinna stand transplantin'.
I'll bate a shilling, when ye're there,
Ye'll rally in your native air."

81

A week's gane by; the maitter's settled,
I'm comin' hame: I'm better fettled,
Fresher lookin', no' sae yallow, —
That doctor chield's a clever fallow.
However, Tam, 'tween me and you,
To shame the deil and say what's true,
My trouble's been — the greater pairt —
A rush o' Ettrick at the hairt.
Ye think I shouldna fashed mysel'
Wi' thoughts o' hame, but nane can tell
What little things may yet torment ye
Till ance ye've left them a' ahint ye.
My hairt, though ye may ca' me fule,
It's a' in Ettrick but the hule.
The country here's a perfit staw,
It's no' the least like oors ava;
A level plain without a bend on't,
Wi' nae beginnin' and nae end on't;
As fer's the eye can look upon,
The land's as flat's a barley-scone.
It's no' like oors, wi' heichs and howes,
Wi' shelter'd neuks and grassy knowes.
The water tae, sae douf and dule,
No' here a stream and there a pule;
Until ye test it wi' a straw,
Ye hardly ken it moves ava.

Ah, Tam! gie me a Border burn
That canna rin without a turn,
And wi' its bonnie babble fills
The glens amang oor native hills.
How men that ance have ken'd aboot it
Can leeve their after lives without it,
I canna tell, for day and nicht
It comes unca'd for to my sicht.
I see't this moment, plain as day,
As it comes bickerin' o'er the brae,

82

Atween the clumps o' purple heather,
Glistenin' in the summer weather,
Syne divin' in below the grun',
Where, hidden frae the sicht and sun,
It gibbers like a deed man's ghost
That clamours for the licht it's lost,
Till oot again the loupin' limmer
Comes dancin' doon through shine and shimmer
At headlang pace, till wi' a jaw
It jumps the rocky waterfa',
And cuts sic cantrips in the air,
The picture-pentin' man's despair;
A rountree bus' oot o'er the tap o't,
A glassy pule to kep the lap o't,
While on the brink the blue harebell
Keeks o'er to see its bonnie sel',
And sittin' chirpin' a' its lane
A water-waggy on a stane.
Ay, penter lad, thraw to the wund
Your canvas, this is holy grund:
Wi' a' its highest airt acheevin',
The picter's deed, and this is leevin'.
When at my warst, my sairest plichts
Took aye the form o' sleepless nichts.
Then what mair nat'ral than look back,
And wander o'er the beaten track?
Sae in my mind, when a' was mirk,
I just begude wi' Ettrick Kirk.
Eh man! I like yon bonnie corner —
For bieldiness it's maist byor'ner.
If back again to Ettrick spared,
Believe me, Tam, in yon kirkyaird
I'd rather lie within the year
Than be Methuselah oot here.
It's weel, when through this vale o' tears,
To think we'll lie wi' oor forebears;
To have oor ain folk side by side

Mak's daith itsel' less ill to bide;
And could we rest wi' hairts mair leal
Than Jamie Hogg and Tibbie Shiel,
And mony mair we baith could name,
As dear, though little ken'd to fame?

Then in my mind I tak' a turn
Frae Thirlestane House to Rankleburn.
On tufty Tushielaw's hillside
The thick-ribbed ruins still abide
Where Adam Scott, that menseless thief —
Scourge o' the Border — cam' to grief.
But I must up and off again,
By Crosslee, Newburgh, Deloraine,
And doon through Hyndhope and the Shaws,
Past bonnie hazel banks and haws,
To Singlie burn; the spot near by
Where Jamie Telfer lost his kye,
Till wi' the help o' bold Buccleuch
And Wat o' Harden's retinue
They soucht a prey wi' muckle speed,
Twice coontit, back to fair Dodhead,
And show'd Bewcastle's bold bravado
The metal Ettrick men were made o'.

And then, is there a bonnier bit
On ony water, head to fit,
Where, tumblin' doon the rugged streams,
The lashin' water froths and creams,
Till o'er the saumon-loup it spins
'Tween green Helmburn and Kirkhope linns,
Where Ettrick rins?
                        Then past Brigend
And fair Howford it tak's a bend,
And wanders through wi' gentler turn
The quiet haughs o' Hutlerburn;
Then on its way it gi'es a ca'
At Fauldshope, Aikwood, Carterha',

Where fairy-fettered young Tamlane
Through Love's great pow'r was freed again.
And noo we've brocht oor wanderin' feet
To where the Forest waters meet,
Where Yarrow's sorrow-laden sang,
That 'mong her hills has linger't lang,
At length yields up her soul — at rest,
A maiden on her lover's breast.

That meeting-pule to me was dear,
I mind its waters deep and clear;
I've fish't it often as a callant,
Wi' muckle zeal and little talent.
The native floo'rs, the auld-worlt stories,
The lyric love, the Border forays,
It's whisperin' eddies, ins and oots,
Spak' ever mair to me than troots.
Fair Water! fairer though it be
Clad in its daithless minstrelsy.
Yet though its sang shall never wane,
It has a beauty o' its ain:
I see its banks, I hear its voices,
As wanderin' onward it rejoices,
And though its music's far frae me,
And though I ken it canna be,
The tear my een a moment blin's,
I hear the linties in the whins
Where Ettrick rins.         But there, I'm dune.
D. V. I'll hae a crack w' 'e sune.
The wife sends love to you and yours.
I'm glad to say we're leavin' oors
Contentit, doin' weel, and happy.
There's plenty room here; naething scrappy.
If man's chief end be gatherin' gear,
There's nae doubt ye can mak' it here.
But post-time's up, sae I'm awa.
Fareweel, and joy be wi' ye a'.

85

# DEATH IN YARROW

### J. B. Selkirk

It's no' the sax month gane
    Sin' a' our cares began —
Sin' she left us here alane,
    Her callant and gudeman.
It was in the spring she dee'd,
    And noo we're in the fa';
And sair we've struggled wi't,
    Sin' his mother gaed awa'.

An awfu' blow was that —
    The deed that nane can dree;
And lang and sair we grat
    For her we couldna see.
I've aye been strong and fell,
    And can stand a gey bit thraw;
But the laddie's no' hissel
    Sin' his mother gaed awa'.

In a' the water-gate
    Ye couldna find his marrow —
There wasna ane his mate
    In Ettrick Shaws or Yarrow.
But he hasna noo the look
    He used to hae ava;
He's grown sae little buik
    Sin' his mother gaed awa'.

I tak' him on my back
    In ilka blink o' sun,
Rin roun' about the stack,
    And mak' believe it's fun.
But weel he kens, I warrant,
    There's something wrang for a',
He's turned sae auld-farrant
    Sin' his mother gaed awa'.

For when he's played his fill,
    I canna help but see
How he draws the creepie-stool
    Aye the closer to my knee;
And he turns his muckle een
    To the picter on the wa',
Wi' a face grown thin and keen,
    Sin' his mother gaed awa'.

I mak' his pickle meat —
    And I think I mak' it weel;
And I warm his little feet,
    When I hap him i' the creel;
And he kisses me fu' couthie,
    For he downa sleep at a'
Till he hauds up his bit mouthie,
    Sin' his mother gaed awa'.

And then I dander oot,
    When I can do nae mair,
And walk the hills aboot,
    I dinna aye ken where;
For my hairt's wi' ane abune,
    And the ane is growin' twa,
He's dwined sae sair, sae sune,
    Sin' his mother gaed awa'.

And noo the lang day's dune,
    And the nicht's begun to fa',
And a bonnie harvest mune
    Rises up on Bourhope Law.
It's a bonnie warlt this,
    But it's no' for me at a',
For a' thing's gane amiss
    Sin' his mother gaed awa'.

# AN APPEAL FROM YARROW*

*J. B. Selkirk*

And is it true? And will they come
   With pick and spade and barrow,
To dig a grave beneath the hills
   For thy dear waters, Yarrow?

Where Scott and Wordsworth sang the songs
   Whose echoes still are ringing;
The valley where "the Shepherd" heard
   His deathless "skylark" singing, —

Oh, touch it not; it fills the heart
   With memories that harrow,
To think that we shall hear no more
   Thy babbling music, Yarrow.

Where every step is holy ground,
   Enshrined in Border story;
Here, sacred to a lover's vows,
   And there, to battle gory.

Where, down by Deuchar's dowie houms,
   The bravest knight in Yarrow
Fell, fighting on the bloody sward,
   All for his "winsome marrow".

Where Cockburn's widow sat beside
   Her murdered hero weeping,
"The moul' upon his yellow hair"
   Her woman's fingers heaping.

*\*Written whilst a Bill to supply Edinburgh
and district with water taken from Yarrow
was before Parliament*

88

Where Margaret and her lover fled —
    Black Douglas and the seven
On ringing hoofs behind them roared
    Their mad appeals to heaven.

Where not a stream that glides between
    Gray rocks with mosses hoary,
But seems to babble to the air
    The burden of its story.

The Lake! oh let not that be made
    A thing of pipes and sluices;
Let something live for beauty's sake,
    Unmixed with baser uses.

Still let it live in fancy's heart,
    A haunt for happy fairies,
And make no wretched reservoir
    Of lovely lone St Mary's.

Disturb not thou its silent deeps,
    Nor yet its gleaming shallows,
The heavenly rest upon its breast,
    The memories it hallows.

The place is more to us than you,
    Who have been goers, comers;
For we have lived our lives in it —
    Its winters and its summers.

We knew it all when we were young,
    And that sets memory sighing,
For now, with bairns about our knees,
    The valley where we're dying.

Oh, touch it not! but let it be
    As nature has arrayed it;
As softening time has sanctified,
    And poet's fancy made it.

A vale where world-worn weary feet
  May come to rest or roam in;
Where pilgrim love has found so much,
  And *we* have found a home in.

*The Bear Gates
Traquair House*

# SELKIRK AFTER FLODDEN
*A widow's dirge, October 1513*

*J. B. Selkirk*

It's but a month the morn
    Sin' a' was peace and plenty;
Oor hairst was halflins shorn,
    Eident men, and lasses denty.
But noo it's a' distress —
    Never mair a merry meetin';
For half the bairns are faitherless,
    And a' the women greetin'.
             O Flodden Field!

Miles and miles round Selkirk toun,
    Where forest flow'rs are fairest,
Ilka lassie's stricken doun,
    Wi' the fate that fa's the sairest.
A' the lads they used to meet
    By Ettrick braes or Yarrow
Lyin' thrammelt head and feet
    In Brankstone's deadly barrow!
             O Flodden Field!

Frae every cleuch and clan
    The best o' the braid Border
Rose like a single man
    To meet the royal order.
Oor Burgh toun itsel'
    Sent its seventy doun the glen;
Ask Fletcher* how they fell,
    Bravely fechting, ane to ten!
             O Flodden Field!

*\* The man who brought an English
flag back to Selkirk from Flodden.
Four brothers of that name are said
to have perished in the battle.*

91

Round about their gallant king,
    For countrie and for croon,
Stude the dauntless Border ring,
    Till the last was hackit doun.
I blame na what has been —
    They maun fa' that canna flee —
But oh, to see what I hae seen,
    To see what now I see!
                O Flodden Field!

The souters a' fu' croose,
    O'er their leather and their lingle,
Wi' their shoon in ilka hoose,
    Sat contentit round the ingle.
Noo there's neathing left but dool, —
    Never mair their wark will cheer them;
In Flodden's bluidy pool
    They'll naether walt nor wear them!
                O Flodden Field!

Whar the weavers used to meet,
    In ilka bieldy corner,
Noo there's nane in a' the street,
    Savin' here and there a mourner,
Walkin' lanely as a wraith,
    Or if she meet anither,
Just a word below their braith
    O' some slauchtered son or brither!
                O Flodden Field!

There stands the gudeman's loom
    That used tae gang sae cheerie,
Untentit noo, and toom,
    Makin' a' the hoose sae eerie,
Till the sicht I canna dree;
    For the shuttles lyin' dumb
Speak the loudlier to me
    O' him that wunna come.
                O Flodden Field!

Sae at nicht I cover't o'er,
    Just to haud it frae my een,
But I haena yet the pow'r
    To forget what it has been;
And I listen through the hoose
    For the chappin' o' the lay,
Till the scrapin' o' a moose
    Tak's my very braith away.
                O Flodden Field!

Then I turn to sister Jean,
    And my airms aboot her twine,
And I kiss her sleepless een,
    For her heart's as sair as mine, —
A heart ance fu' o' fun,
    And hands that ne'er were idle,
Wi' a' her cleedin' spun
    Against her Jamie's bridal.
                O Flodden Field!

Noo we've naether hands nor hairt —
    In oor grief the wark's forgotten,
Tho' it's wantit every airt,
    And the craps are lyin' rotten.
War's awesome blast's gane by,
    And left a land forlorn;
In daith's dool hairst they lie,
    The shearers an' the shorn.
                O Flodden Field!

Wi' winter creepin near us,
    When the nichts are drear an' lang,
Nane to help us, nane to hear us,
    On the weary gate we gang!
Lord o' the quick an' deed,
    Sin' oor ain we canna see,
In mercy mak gude speed,
    And bring us whar they be,
                Far, far frae Flodden Field!

# ROGER QUIN (1850–1925)

## POET AND BOHEMIAN

*Roger Quin was a poet by hereditary right. His father was a poet before him, and had considerable standing as such in the south of Scotland: he produced a volume entitled* The Heather Lintie *which ran to three hundred pages. Roger was born on June 25th, 1850, the only son in a family of twelve. The house in which he was born overlooked the graveyard where Robert Burns was buried.*

*While his father worked in turn as a weaver and stonebreaker, Roger was sent to Dumfries Academy by a benefactor, and there he excelled. After leaving school he worked in the Town Clerk's office in Dumfries and later became a railway clerk at Silloth. Restless, he moved to Glasgow and then Galashiels, where his father was employed as a travelling bookseller. Roger worked in local factories and wrote some drama and poetry, but was happier walking the countryside and fishing its rivers. His poem "The Borderland" was first recognised south of the border rather than at home (as is so often the case). Another poem, with the incongruous title "A Skylark Singing over Barnhill Poorhouse", received attention in turn, but Roger Quin shunned the conventional life and took to the road like a tramp, and many a time played his tin whistle for his supper. He was equally at home in a cave he knew at Wigtown Bay, or, wrapped up in an old cloak, sleeping rough beside Hogg's monument at the head of Yarrow. He loved to cast a line over a rising trout, and lie by an open fire at night with a drum o' tea and the fish sizzling in a pan.*

*Then kindly friends furnished a wee cottage for him at the Yair, beside the river and near to Selkirk and Galashiels. Like Scott's Minstrel before him, he could sit in his own "newark" with his muse and fish the streams to his heart's content.*

A simple rough-hewn memorial stone can be seen where Quin so enthused about "Scotland's Eden from the spur o' Gala Hill", a place well known to the local people for its beauty and quietness.

Flodden Field

# THE BORDERLAND

*Roger Quin*

From the moorland and the meadows
To this city of the shadows,
Where I wander old and lonely, comes the call I understand;
In clear, soft tones enthralling,
It is calling — calling — calling —
'Tis the Spirit of the Open from the dear old Borderland!

Ah that call! who can gainsay it?
To hear is to obey it;
I must leave the bustling city to the busy city men —
Leave behind its feverish madness,
It's scenes of sordid sadness;
And drink the unpolluted air of Yarrow once again!

For the grim, huge city daunts me,
Its wail of sorrow haunts me —
A nameless Atom tossed amidst the human surf that beats!
For ever and for ever,
In a frenzy of endeavour,
Along the cruel barriers of its never-ending streets!

I shall leave it in the morning —
Just slip out without a warning,
Save a hand-clasp to the friend who knows the call that
lures me on;
In the city's clang and clatter
One old man the less won't matter;
And no one here will say me nay, or care that I am gone.

What tho' my wallet's meagre?
That won't quell my spirit eager —
Like careless-hearted Goldsmith when he wandered by the Po,

Whichever way I turn me,
My simple flute will earn me
In the kindly Border country, food and shelter as I go.

I shall see old Neidpath hoary,
With its dim, romantic story,
And soon have glimpses through the trees of ghostly grey Traquair;
And in my happy wand'ring
Adown the Tweed's meand'ring
Shall note the Peel, and Ashiestiel, and onward to the Yair.

By Caddonfoot I'll linger —
It has charms to stay the singer —
And from the bridge a painter's dream of beauty then I'll see;
But I'll leave it there behind me,
Ere the evening shadows find me
Passing the vines at Clovenfords to haunted Torwoodlee.

Gala Water shall not hold me —
Tho' its mem'ries fair enfold me —
Nor many-gabled Abbotsford, so stately and so still;
For I'll hasten to the vision
Of a valley fair, Elysian,
And gaze on Scotland's Eden from the spur of Gala Hill.

Ah me! shall I recapture
The early joyous rapture
Which shook my being's pulses when that scene first met my eye?
Steeped in old Border story
It stretched in radiant glory,
To where the filmy Cheviots hung along the southern sky!

Fair Dryburgh and Melrose,
Touched by the Wizard's spell, rose,
And Bemersyde, and Leaderfoot, and Elwyn's Fairy Dene:
The Tweed serenely gliding,
Now seen — now coyly hiding,
While Eildon raised his triple crest, and sentinelled the scene!

The spell — the dream is over:
I awake, but to discover
The city's rush — the jostling crowds — the din on every hand;
But, on my ear soft falling,
I can hear the curlews calling,
And I know that soon I'll see them in the dear old Borderland!

*St Mary's Loch
& The Loch o' The Lowes*

# MIDNIGHT IN YARROW

*Roger Quin*

Sport of the Fates! it comes about
   A wanderer has been hither hurled;
A human foam-flake flung from out
   The madd'ning maelstrom of the world!

What makes he here — this homeless tramp?
   No tripper's sleek content is his,
Whose furrowed features bear the stamp
   Of pleasure's sad antithesis.

No tourist this, with feelings blent,
   Who — inly glad — here fain would grieve;
Trying a fresh experiment:
   The luxury of make-believe;

Nor poet of the facile pen,
   Word spinning in a reek divine,
Which floats about his cosy den,
   From fumes of after-dinner wine;

But one who, far from fashion's train,
   Follows the call that lures him on,
In Nature's arms to soothe his pain;
   In Yarrow's sadness lose his own.

Child of the old Earth Mother, he
   Has wandered far from street and mart;
And here — in her own sanctuary —
   Creeps closer to the mother's heart.

# WILLIAM HENRY OGILVIE (1869– ? )

POET AND JOURNALIST

*He was not a man who wrote from the cosy atmosphere of leather-bound books and a warm fire. William Henry Ogilvie wrote from the raw materials of life; he did not live in a vacuum: his roots were deep down in mother earth. Born at Holefield, Kelso in 1869, W. H. O. was educated at Fettes College, Edinburgh. He went to Australia in 1889, where he spent eleven years in the bush, sampling sheep station life, returning to his native heath in 1900.*

*When in Australia, he wrote an enormous amount of poetry. The volume* Fair Girls and Grey Horses *was very gallant stuff for a hard fighting, hard living country.* Rainbows and Witches *followed, and* Saddle for a Throne, *which shows how a man could come to terms with his environment and, despite drought and loss, overcome it: "The swamps were dry, the creek was low," but he could still feel for the horses and cattle, and the swagman forbye.*

*W. H. O. was much admired in Australia, and elsewhere, though it may be true to say he pleased the public better than the critics. Some of his work appeared from time to time in* Punch *and other magazines, and he was for about two years Professor of Agricultural Journalism in the United States. He died at a ripe old age in his native Borderland.*

# KELSO BRIDGE

*W. H. Ogilvie*

There is one spot where memory guides
    From time to time my restless heart —
A fair, fair spot, where silver tides
    Break on grey piers and drift apart
Round pillars spun with water-weed,
    Down channels where the foam is whirled;
So beats my love of home, O Tweed!
    Against the barriers of the world!

Sunlit or swept by winter's blast
    The old bridge stands, a link between
The Abbey's hoar and wrinkled past
    And the young elm-bud's waking green;
The nesting rooks above it wheel
    From elm to elm on sable wings;
Beneath it, racing round the reel,
    The line upon the bent rod sings.

Across the world hope's bridges bear
    The wanderer's never-resting feet,
But peace and rest are mingled where
    Earth's fairest rivers, mingling, meet.
On pillars twined with water-weed
    Your silver tide is ceaseless hurled;
So beats my love of home, O Tweed!
    Against the barriers of the world!

# THE MARCH BURN

*W. H. Ogilvie*

Folk will tell you in their order,
    Bowmont, Teviot, Tweed in turn;
But I know the real Border,
    And I know the true March Burn.

'Tis the playground of the swallow,
    'Tis the heron's banquet-hall,
Just a gleam the wild ducks follow
    When the evening shadows fall.

Just a strip of sunny water
    That a man may step across,
Just a little laughing daughter
    Of the mist-cloud and the moss.

Meadow-sweet and hemlock love her,
    And when soft the South wind blows
There are kisses blown above her
    From the thistle to the rose.

And, though Tweed may claim the honour,
    She who dances through the fern
With the white lace-foam upon her
    Is the true March Burn.

# TILL THE KING RETURNS

*W. H. Ogilvie*

The wild rose twines on the gateway there,
   The green weed grows and the bramble clings,
Barring the road to thy hearth, Traquair,
   With the loyal hands of the earth's green things;
The wind through the rusted iron sings,
   The sun on the self-sown tangle burns,
But never a hoof on the roadway rings —
   The gate is shut till the King returns.

I had a lover, gallant and fair —
   Ah! nought but sorrow the memory brings! —
I opened my heart to him, everywhere,
   He was my guest, and his right a king's;
But lightly his love at the last took wings
   Flying away with the hawks and herns,
And a gate no more on its hinges swings —
   My heart is shut till my King returns.

# THE COMFORT OF THE HILLS

*W. H. Ogilvie*

Heart! If you've a sorrow
    Take it to the hills!
Lay it where the sunshine
    Cups of colour spills!
Hide it in the shadow
    Of the folding fern;
Bathe it in the coolness
    Of the brown hill burn;
Give it to the west wind
    Blowing where it wills;
Heart! If you've a sorrow
    Take it to the hills!

Heart! If you've a sorrow
    Take it to the hills!
Where pity crowns the silence
    And love the loneness fills!
Bury it in bracken
    Waving green and high;
O'er it let the heather's
    Peaceful purple lie!
Trust it to the healing
    Heaven itself distils;
Heart! If you've a sorrow
    Take it to the hills!

# THE HARP OF ETTRICK

*W. H. Ogilvie*

In a green kirkyard where the silent hills
    Are a guard to the glamour that Ettrick keeps,
Rocked by the music of rain-fed rills
    The shepherd friend of the fairies sleeps.
Nought nameth his grave the rest among,
    Save the simple slab as a headstone set,
With the deep-cut date when he lived and sung,
    And a carven harp — lest the world forget!
Round him the sheep and the moorfowl feed,
    Close to his shoulder the heathbells blow,
And the sun may shine and he does not heed,
    And the flowers may bloom and he does not know.

But at night, when the arras of cloud is torn
    And tossed by the Solway winds aside,
When the moon comes sailing above Delorne
    And sets in her silver the Ettrick tide,
When the magic wing of the midnight hour
    Stoops low to the worn old Gamescleuch walls,
And a lonely owl on the Thirlestane Tower
    With a querulous note to the silence calls,
Then a murmur wakes in the heath and fern,
    And the fairies gather, unseen of men,
Riding up from the Rankleburn
    And trooping down from the Tima Glen.

So soft is the fall of their feet in the grass,
  So light is the lift of each gossamer wing,
You might think it the murmur of breezes that pass
  Leaving whispers of love on the lips of the ling.
They cross the low Ettrick by light of the moon
  That has robed in her lilies the foam on its wave,
They climb the dark dyke where the shadows are strewn,
  And stand with bowed heads on the marge of his grave.
However so soft be their step, he has heard,
  And he moves to their midst like a king to his throne,
Not a leaf, not a blade in the grasses is stirred
  As he lifts the grey harp from its place on the stone.

The dead strings waken beneath his hand,
  And the echoes ring through the cleuch and ford,
As he sings of a new Kilmeny's land
  And a new Earl Walter's matchless sword;
'Tis a song that is never for mortal ear,
  And the grave to the world is unstirred and still,
And he who might pass by the kirk would hear
  No sound but the wind as it crossed on the hill;
Yet those golden words to the vale belong,
  And the tale is a tale that the fairies know,
And the wail of that harp is the deathless song
  That the dreamer hears in the Ettrick's flow.

# SMAILHOLM TOWER

*W. H. Ogilvie*

Here by the peel-tower old and grey
   In the sunlit mornings a lame boy lay,
Speeding his thought o'er ridge and tree
   To the magic peaks of the Eildons three;
Hearing the raider's battle-cry
   In the call of the whaup that wandered by;
Filling his heart with patriot pride
   From the far-flung fields of the Borderside.

The birds flew high; and the lad was lame;
   Yet his step was sure in the fields of Fame;
And the lagging foot has changed to wings
   That have beckoned nations and gladdened kings;
And the lilt he learned from the larks above
   Has been woven in songs of war and love,
And twined into stories sweet and grand
   To the lasting pride of the Borderland.

From Sandy Knowe as the winds blow down
   Over Bemersyde into Melrose Town,
Laden with love they will turn aside
   To the silent tomb by the silver tide,
With a borrowed note from the years of old
   Of wild birds crying above the wold,
And the scent of thorn and moorland flower
   When a boy lay dreaming by Smailholm Tower.

We have built him statues in street and square,
   We have carved him a temple rich and rare,
But the grandest stone to his memory still
   Is a grey-walled tower on the windy hill;
For there, long since, in a golden morn
   Was the glamour shaped and the glory born
That marked a path for the Master's pen
   And drew the chains on a world of men.

# THE DEIL'S MITTEN

*W. H. Ogilvie*

To keep the deil busy, long since they decreed
   He should build them at Kelso a cauld on the Tweed.
He builded in haste, and he builded alone
   Till half the grey river was girded with stone;
And he gathered the boulders from near and afar
   But had never enough for the breadth of the bar.
So he spread his black wings over steeple and tree
   And he carried a load every night from the sea;
Oh, he carried them swift and he carried them sure,
   One load every night over lone Lammermoor.

One night as he rose from the rocks of Dunbar,
   There was never a glint of a moon or a star,
Yet, so well did he know every turn of the way
   He had won to the Tweed ere the breaking of day.
But at the back of Byrecleuch he was flying so fast
   That he scratched just one hand on the crag as he passed.
It was little he cared, it was nothing to feel,
   And anyway what is a scratch to the deil? —
But as ill-luck would have it, his mitten was rent
   And the stones that he carried tipped over and went
And the roar of their fall as the records attest
   Was heard many miles to the east and the west —
At the back of Byrecleuch, by the crag on the hill,
   The stones the deil carried are waiting him still.